WORDS TO TRUST

For Jennifer Aitken
with warmest good wishes
and every blessing

Campbell Gillon

June 1994

Contents

Acknowledgments

The influence of many people and books upon me over forty years of ministry I gratefully acknowledge, with particular mention of Professor William Barclay, renowned New Testament scholar and interpreter, my outstanding teacher at Trinity College, Glasgow. To those loyal friends, old and new in Scotland and in America, who have shared in my ministry, I am greatly indebted.

From the moment the idea of this book was conceived, its preparation has been a cooperative venture with my wife, Audrey, and with our close friend Dorothy Fosdick. They have my deep thanks. Skillfully transcribed by Audrey from the original tapes, the sermons were on hand for a selection. With Dorothy's enheartening counsel, energy, and expertise, the final manuscript took shape for publication.

I also want to record with gratitude the exceptional thoughtfulness of my publisher, Jed Lyons, and his gifted staff, especially Lynn Gemmell, in the production of this volume.

As will be evident, I have freely used several different translations of the Bible: the King James, the Moffatt, the New English Bible, the Revised Standard Version, J. B. Phillips, among others. Each has its insight.

WORDS TO TRUST

Campbell Gillon

Barnes & Noble Books
Lanham, Maryland

———

T & T Clark
Edinburgh, Scotland

First published in the United States of America in 1991 by
BARNES & NOBLE BOOKS
8705 Bollman Place, Savage, Maryland 20763

Published in the United Kingdom in 1991 by
T&T Clark Ltd.
59 George Street, Edinburgh, Scotland EH2 2LQ

Library of Congress Cataloging-in-Publication Data

Gillon, Campbell.
Words to Trust / by Campbell Gillon.
p.   cm.
1. Presbyterian Church—Sermons.
2. Sermons, American.
I. Title.
BX9178.G48W67 1991
252' .051—dc20   91-26428 CIP

ISBN 0–389–20948–1 (cloth : alk. paper)
ISBN 0–389–20949–X (pbk. : alk. paper)

British Cataloging in Publication Information

T & T Clark Ltd.

ISBN 0-567-09600-9 (cloth: alk. paper)
ISBN 0-567-29203-7 (pbk.: alk. paper)

Printed in the United States of America

 TM The paper used in this publication meets the minimum requirements of
American National Standard for Information Sciences—Permanence of
Paper for Printed Library Materials, ANSI Z39.48–1984.

*With love
for my wife, Audrey
who constantly combines
fun and faith
delight and duty
the ideal and the real*

Introduction

In April 1980 I preached my last sermon as a minister of the Church of Scotland, packed my kilt, and left for the "New World." I had accepted the call of the Georgetown Presbyterian Church in Washington, D.C., a landmark congregation founded in 1780 and noted for the longest unbroken ministry of Christian witness and service in the nation's capital. I have been privileged to speak from the pulpit of that historic church for over a decade.

In the Bible we find words to trust: the good news of God's power to strengthen and save us in the face of trouble, sin, and death. Proclaiming this is a daunting but divine commission. To use the biblical metaphor, the eternal Word is a two-edged sword which should be handled with care and respect. Honed by reverent scholarship, it should not be misused as a bludgeon of literalism, or turned into a bow for launching the speculative arrows of one's own agenda. It is a blade fashioned for the searching cut and thrust of God's spirit piercing through all human armor to our inmost being, evoking a response in our minds, hearts, and lives.

A D.C. cabbie, the Attorney General, women executives, a Cambodian refugee, teachers, university students, scientists, homemakers, and a Ford dealership owner are part of the broad spectrum of the week-by-week congregation. With this kind of encouragement, I have gathered in the present volume my attempts to address some of the great central themes of the Christian faith. I believe this faith speaks to the deepest needs and highest motives of men and women in today's world. While ministers, teachers of religion, and seminary students may find this book useful, it is primarily for individuals in all walks of life, young and old, who are facing life's strains, encountering its temptations, and yearning to fulfill its possibilities.

Because what follows was originally spoken discourse, I ask the reader to listen for the Word within the words.

Campbell Gillon,
Washington, D.C.

"Here are words you may trust. . . ."

Paul—1 Timothy 1:15

I

The Nature of God

1

It all depends what you mean by . . .

Three-Letter Word

Home from church, someone was asked at the lunch table what the minister had preached about. "He preached about God and about twenty minutes!" she replied. That is exactly what I propose to do today.

I realize it may sound presumptuous to attempt to pin down anything of the Infinite in a matter of minutes. It is like trying to discourse on the ocean with a glass of seawater in your hand for illustration. But if that small amount of water is analyzed, a great deal can be learned about the essential nature and composition of the ocean and the life it can support. God is infinitely greater than any ocean. Yet if we grasp something of His essential nature, we have vital knowledge.

Now "God" is a three-letter word which covers a multitude of conceptions and misconceptions. "So you believe in God?" says one man to another. In the speaker's mind is the image of a celestial Santa Claus who is there to reward the good people and find out who's been naughty or nice. Such a God, rightly enough, he cannot tolerate. This, however, may not at all be the idea of God in the mind of the person addressed. His God may be quite different: an

3

infinite Being bent on righteousness, justice, and truth, with whom he has a relationship of dependence, trust, obedience, and love. And so the same word, "God," is shot down or upheld, depending upon the content people give to it and their ideas behind it.

Define your terms: it all depends what you mean by "God."

*
* *

Let us make sure we are talking of the same thing. If ever there was a word about which that needed to be said, it is this three-letter word. It all depends what you mean by "God."

There are countless men and women living in the world today without any faith in God. Not because they are especially bad, selfish, or godless, but because they have not found with their adult minds a God big enough to account for life; big enough to fit in with scientific discoveries; big enough to command their highest admiration and respect.

It is usually thought that the Church's inherited idea of God goes back to the old Hebrew conception born in an ancient land where people visualized a three-decker universe—a kind of cosmic "Whopper" or "Big Mac"—with the earth (flat) in the middle, Sheol (the place of the dead) on the lower level, and the heavens a few miles "somewhere up there." Of course, we understand that the earth is round and "up" and "down" are relative terms. God can no longer be crudely thought of as Someone "up there" or Someone "out there."

It has been argued that if in our modern world God is to be credible and intelligible, people must grasp a new and more adequate idea of Him. And so God has been described in this century as "the ground of our being"—a concept of startling dullness and impersonality. I am sure that whatever else God is, He is neither dull nor impersonal. More than personal, perchance; certainly not less.

I feel that convinced Christians who have their own ideas of God based on experience and the words of Christ are often a bit startled when they hear of theologians' way-out ideas of God expressed in new and unfamiliar images. Not for a moment would I suggest that we rush to replace our ideas of God—made real through experience in the day of trouble and the hour of darkness—with unfamiliar modern concepts. But I would ask that whether we are traditional believers or avant-garde theologians, we realize that we are dealing with a God greater than anybody's idea—or everybody's idea—of Him: a God who can never be neatly defined, pigeonholed, and done with as changing circumstances or increased knowledge renders Him obsolete.

That thought is admirably conveyed in Exodus 3:14 in the margin of the Revised Standard Version: "And God said unto Moses, 'I will be what I will be.' " This is an alternative translation of the better-known phrase, "I am what I am," and seems to fit the situation more aptly.

God, revealing Himself to Moses in the wilderness, commissions him to lead the Israelites out of bondage in Egypt. Moses is extremely reluctant. "Who am I that I should go unto Pharaoh and bring forth the Children of Israel out of Egypt?" "Certainly I will be with thee," God assures him. But Moses is not yet persuaded. "Behold," he says, "when I come unto the people and shall say to them, 'The God of your fathers hath sent me to you,' they shall say to me, 'What is His name?' What shall I say to them?"

Remember that among the Hebrews the name of a person was thought to reveal that individual's character. So something vital happens when there is a change of name. "Jacob," for example, means "supplanter" which connotes his taking the rightful place of his brother Esau. Later, after his struggles, Jacob is given the new name "Israel" meaning

"Prince of God." Thus, Moses wanted a name for God: a definition of God to sum up His nature.

But God cannot be summed up in a word, not even the word "Love." It all depends upon what you mean by "Love"—and God is too big to be shut within the limits of mere words.

If Moses looked for a present-tense definition of God, what he got for an answer was in the future tense. "I will be what I will be," says God. That is His name. He is greater than the ideas of any generation. The Divine Nature is that which from time to time His obedient people discover it to be, each age learning more.

God's answer carries a challenge. For God says in effect to Moses:

> Tell the people that I am a God who grows, or rather, a God of whom your knowledge will grow. I stand before you like a great mountain, forever the same, yet as you climb in trust each higher vantage point will give you an ever-widening view of My nature. I do not merely say that I am what I am, or that I will be what I have been. I tell you, I will be what you will discover Me to be as I meet your future unknown needs. I will be what I will be.

*
**

The problem of religion is always to achieve a worthier conception of God. There is no such problem with a dead religion. A living faith, however, continuously seeks more adequate ideas of God. Follow the amazing story of the development of the idea of God in the Judeo-Christian tradition.

In primitive fashion, the Hebrews begin their idea of God as One very like a man—anthropomorphic—walking in a garden in the cool of the day, looking for Adam in Eden. Then, like the Greeks with their god Zeus on Mount Olympus, Jehovah becomes associated with Mount Sinai— yet with several vital differences. The God of the Hebrews does not play games with mortals. He lays down laws for living in community; laws of reverence and respect which are still relevant today and which we neglect at our peril.

Time passes. The Jews are in Palestine. No longer is Jehovah confined to distant Mount Sinai. He is there filling the Land of Promise. Yet He is thought to be geographically limited. Other gods for other countries! This is the significance of Ruth's words when, coming from the land of Moab where she had always worshiped Moab's god, Chemosh, she says to Naomi, "Thy people shall be my people and thy God, my God. . . ." Change countries and change gods! Leave the old deity in the old dominion.

Ages roll and communications increase. Jehovah is now seen to be the God of all the earth. Isaiah says, "It is He who sitteth above the circle of the earth and all the inhabitants are as grasshoppers." It is still a three-decker universe with heaven above and the place of the dead, Sheol, below. What has God to do with these? Says the Psalmist in one of the most magnificent enlargements of the idea of God in human thought:

> If I ascend up into Heaven, Thou art there:
> If I make my bed in Sheol, behold, Thou art there;
> If I take the wings of the morning,
> And dwell in the uttermost parts of the sea;
> Even there shall Thy hand lead me,
> And Thy right hand shall hold me. . . .

After centuries, the early Christian tradition moves into the Greek world of philosophical ideas. But the people do not give up God, they expand their understanding of Him.

Paul proclaims on Mars hill: "He is not far from anyone of us. In Him we live and move. In Him we exist." John writes: "In the beginning was the Word—the creative Word. The Word was with God, and the Word was God. . . . The Word became flesh and dwelt among us. . . ." The first letter of John declares: "God is Love. He who dwells in Love, dwells in God and God in Him." Supremely, Jesus tells us, "God is a Spirit and those who worship Him must worship Him in spirit and in truth."

We have come a long way from a God who walked in a garden. Still, however, the earth is regarded as the center of the universe with the sun, the moon, and the stars revolving around it—a comparatively cozy place. And then come the shattering discoveries of Copernicus, Galileo, and others. The universe is suddenly a vast place of incredible distance and we discover we are not at its center. Once again human discernment of God develops and grows. Confronting an infinite scheme and a sun-centered system with plants regular in their courses, Joseph Addison, founder of the English magazine *The Spectator*, wrote in 1712:

> The spacious firmament on high
> With all the blue ethereal sky
> And spangled heaven, a shining frame
> Their great Original proclaim. . . .
> Forever singing, as they shine,
> "The hand that made us is divine."

Since then a revolution of scientific revelation has taken place: power, electrical and nuclear; flight across oceans and in space; new knowledge of the human condition; and an information explosion through computers. All these were unknown to previous ages. In the face of this, some people stand looking back and say: "God is gone. God is dead. No longer is He necessary as a hypothesis to fill in the gaps in our knowledge. For these gaps are narrowing. Given time, the human intellect will deprive Him of these hideouts forever."

But the real God is not the God of gaps in knowledge, the God of ignorance and superstition who can be slain with truth. The God and Father of our Lord Jesus Christ is the God of Truth. It is not so much that He grows with the passing of the centuries but that we grow into a deeper understanding of Him. For He is One who reveals more and more of Himself to those who seek Him in spirit and in truth, to those who know that His name is "I will be what I will be." Just as the ocean's essence is in the glass of seawater, so is God's essential nature revealed in Christ.

*
* *

Yet frankly, our finite minds cannot grasp the infinite. The Eternal Being who is behind and beyond, in and through this vast complex of all creation, we cannot comprehend. To express our ideas, we need to use symbol. We take something we know and lift it up as high as we can, using it to help us think about Him. Yet we do not imagine that our best symbol has compassed Him. For still, He will be what He will be. From our human experiences we give the names: a Rock, a Fortress, a Shepherd, a Father, a Mother, a Savior, a Friend.

We Christians say that we have seen in the face of Jesus Christ the light of the knowledge of the glory of God. It is good that we should. For this is the human shore of the eternal ocean that is God. This is what the Divinity of Jesus means: not that all of the great God was in Jesus—the Omnipotence, the Omnipresence, the Omniscience; but that the vital essence of God—the Love, the Goodness, the Truth—was there in Jesus Christ. In His life and death and rising again, millions have discovered a power for victorious living that is beyond human power. They have felt in tune with the Infinite. They have felt the pull of an eternal sea of Love.

We Christians know that this is the God who made us—made us with such depths to our being that they can only be fully called to, and answered by, the depths in Him. Rest assured. This is no childhood deity we coax by prayer to do things our way and then discard with our toys when we think He has let us down. This is the God who in Christ has wrestled with the intractable problems of sin, suffering, and death and solved them through the sacrifice of Himself. This is the God whom we so often sparingly adore in our worship, although His truth in other people has blessed our lives directly or indirectly since the day we were born. This is the God who will bear us up in time and in eternity, no matter what befalls us, by being what He will be—when the day comes.

> O God, our Help in ages past,
>   Our Hope for years to come,
> Be Thou our Guard while life shall last,
>   And our eternal Home.

This is the God we adore who, in as yet unimagined revelations of His Love for us, will be what He will be.

GRACIOUS GOD, open our eyes—the eyes of the soul—to your truth. May we recognize that you do not grow, for you are already great beyond all knowledge. Yet, bit by bit, help us grow spiritually to become mature enough to grasp ever more of you, as did men and women of vision in the long history of our race who saw farther than the rest. Above all, we bless you for revealing yourself in Christ, who hast shown us your essential nature. Help us to know this is constant as we trust you for the future, when we shall experience greater revelations of your unchanging, wondrous Love. AMEN.

2

Divine Initiative

The God Effect

There is one pursuit in which advertisers and hucksters are forever engaged: trying to persuade the buying public that their product makes absolutely all the difference. A glass in your hand and you'll have savoir faire. Wear it on the bald spot and you'll look years younger. Slosh it on the dull, dirty floor and you'll be dazzled by the permanent shine. The emphasis is the same for all. What a difference between the before and after.

Advertising has so conditioned us to expect technological miracles in the superficial and trivial things of life that it almost inoculates us against the one vital "before and after" transformation beyond human devising—that which God can do in those people and with those people who have honest dealings with Him. This is no outcome of mankind's wisdom or self-will, no fruit of meditation technique or esoteric knowledge, but those things "hidden from the wise," as Jesus says in Matthew 11:25, "which God reveals to mere children."

For illustration, here is the archetypal case history of committing to Christ and dying to self—the God effect on

13

the soul—the greatest "before and after" possible. Paul tells
us in Galatians 1:13–16:

> You have heard what my manner of life was when I was
> still a practicing Jew; how savagely I persecuted the
> church of God and tried to destroy it; and how in the
> practice of our national religion I was outstripping
> many of my Jewish contemporaries in my boundless
> devotion to the traditions of my ancestors. But then in
> His good pleasure God, who had set me apart from
> birth and called me through His grace, chose to reveal
> His Son to me and through me, in order that I might
> proclaim Him among the Gentiles.

There you have the vital "before and after" transformation. The passion and the pride done away with; the old
self, dead; a new birth from God who had His eye on Paul
from the beginning. Now in Christ, a new creature; a new
purpose; a new direction.

Through the answers to the following questions, we will
discover the essential ingredients of all such life-shaking
and life-shaping.

***

The first question: How did it happen? The answer is
simple enough to say, yet utterly profound to grasp and
accept: by Divine Initiative.

God acts. He reveals Himself. This revelation is the self-
disclosure of God; showing Himself in a way that no
amount of persistent human searching could ever discover;
being Himself personally active in lifting the veil that blurs
the spiritual vision. When Peter makes his great affirmation
of Jesus as Messiah, Jesus says to him, "Flesh and blood
have not revealed this to you, but My Father in Heaven."

God's revelation is often thought of in a propositional fashion with the Bible as a compendium of divine truths supernaturally and inerrantly communicated to men and women, a series of great principles from which we may construct a system of belief and draft a plan of salvation.

Yet how can human language ever adequately express the inexpressible? How can we describe the majesty and the glory of the infinite Being and His gracious stooping down to us in Christ? The Bible is the record of the Divine Initiative from creation to redemption against the background of human sin. But God does not save the world by authorship. It is His action in reconciliation that makes the new creation, and that action involves the Holy Spirit making dead letters live with meaning until men and women are confronted with the Eternal Word who is from the beginning. Not a series of religious propositions, but that mysterious One who has chosen to give us a glimpse, through inadequate human words, of what He has done.

The Divine Initiative is more than propositional. And it is more than pictorial. We can think of God as allowing Himself to be seen in Christ, much as a mirror-topped table would reflect a magnificent painting on the ceiling. Jesus' words, "He that hath seen me hath seen the Father" would seem an appropriate text. Yet though this pictorial idea of revelation is attractive, it does not do justice to the main message of the New Testament which is not that the glory of the invisible God is mirrored in a man on earth, but that in this person, Jesus Christ, God Himself has uniquely entered the human situation. Thus He gives us not just His portrait or His principle, but His very Presence in saving action.

The Divine Initiative is more than past propositional or illuminating pictorial, it is present personal. It is God in Christ—a divine rescue, not a divine reflection. Here is God in action meeting our sin with His grace which is the extravagant love He has for undeserving humanity. In the Cross of Calvary we see the focal point of the full revelation.

Before such a demonstration of the Divine Initiative, our attitude must be that of Charles Wesley:

> 'Tis mystery all! The Immortal dies!
>   Who can explore His strange design?
> In vain the first-born seraph tries
>   To sound the depths of love divine.
> 'Tis mercy all! let earth adore;
>   Let angel minds inquire no more.

*
**

How does it happen? By Divine Initiative. God reveals Himself in action. As with Paul, so with us. But what happened? A dramatic change. A new life in Christ; a dying to self; the revolution of redemption. On the road to Damascus Paul, as we know, "saw the light."

Like the classical Greeks, we tend to intellectualize the metaphor of light. Light, for us the enlightened, means the difference between knowledge and ignorance. For the men of the Bible, it is the difference between security and danger, the difference between stumbling in the dark— victim of wild beasts and evil doers—and walking in the day, in safety and assurance. "The Lord is my light and my salvation." "The people that walked in darkness have seen a great light." "Arise, shine for thy light is come." For the Hebrew, these are descriptions of divine deliverance, not intellectual insight.

Paul had "thought" himself to a standstill, outstripping his contemporaries in his boundless devotion to the Hebrew faith and practice, savagely persecuting this new sect. He was like a man walking down a long dark road with a distant powerful searchlight often catching his eye. The nearer he goes, the less he sees his way. Suddenly he stops and sees the light as though for the first time. Then he realizes that this is God's light of deliverance which he has tried to avoid by shielding his eyes in order to see where he was going. How blind he has been. Now, with his sight gone, Paul sees.

Mentally, he looks back down the road he has come; his whole life up to the present is now illumined by the light of deliverance. As Paul says in his letter to the Galatians, he is sure that God has set him apart from his birth; called him by His grace; and chosen to reveal Christ to him and through him. Like a dumb ox, he has stubbornly resisted the pointers and the goads that would have led him in God's way. But that is all past. The liberating light of God has delivered him from continuing in his frustrated, stumbling, and sinful way. What he has discarded, he now picks up. What he has hated, he now loves. What he has discounted, he now values. What he has scorned, he now makes central. Those whom he would have killed, he now devotes his life to serving.

Obviously something has happened within Paul that cannot be accounted for in terms of heredity, environment, education, or personal gifts. These are not reasons for such a transformation, but treasures. Treasures not to be obliterated but to be offered to a new Master. "I live," cries Paul, "yet not I. Not the old me. Christ lives in me." This is the God effect. The revolution of redemption means living to Him, dying to self. This Jesus on whose followers Paul thought to lay his hands has laid His hands on him.

Sings the old spiritual, "I know de Lord done laid His hand on me." And that kind of overwhelming wonder which is genuinely staggered at the grace of God is essential for the change I'm talking about. It may happen all at once, in apparently sudden dramatic fashion like Paul's conversion and many others. It may be the gradual growth of the searching soul that is ready when the revelation comes.

A man once wrote a letter to the London *Times* describing how it was his job early each Sunday morning to climb the spire of St. Michael's Church, which crowns Highgate Hill in London, to wind the clock. Often as he looked out from that height he could see nothing, for the clouds and mists hid the view. But other times, the sun pierced the mist and there at his feet lay all the glory of London. "How like the religious life," he added. "We go regularly to church and often nothing seems to happen. But then one morning the mists, as it were, fall apart and the Son of Righteousness arises with healing in His wings."

No words can adequately describe what happens in the soul. We use poetry, analogy, metaphor, and external details of incident to express what is really a profound internal experience. But when we truly encounter God, nothing— absolutely nothing—is ever the same again. In his poem "The Everlasting Mercy," John Masefield depicts Saul Kane, an aggressive, lying reprobate suddenly confronted by God in this kind of experience. Masefield uses words as well as words can be used to describe the result:

> O glory of the lighted mind.
> How dead I'd been, how dumb, how blind.
> The station brook, to my new eyes,
> Was babbling out of Paradise.
> The waters rushing from the rain
> Were singing Christ has risen again.
> I thought all earthly creatures knelt
> From rapture of the joy I felt . . .
> I did not think, I did not strive,
> The deep peace burnt my me alive;
> The bolted door had broken in,
> I knew that I had done with sin.

I knew that Christ had given me birth
To brother all the souls on earth. . . .

*
**

Yes, and Paul knew that too. The hallmark of the genuine experience of God's grace is the practical outcome in life. The Divine Initiative, the present personal revelation that wrought the dramatic change for Paul, the very revolution of redemption was for a purpose: the purpose of redirecting his life—a most evident and vivid outcome. In Masefield's words, he was now "to brother all the souls on earth." Or, as Paul himself put it, "God chose me to reveal His Son to me and through me, in order that I might proclaim Him among the Gentiles." If Romans 8 or 1 Corinthians 13 has ever made any kind of impact on you, you are part of the practical outcome of Paul's living to Christ and dying to self—his redirected life.

In the course of my ministry many students and other young people have come to see me who do not really know where they are going or where their life's work lies. In talking with them, I have found myself offering two pointers from my own experience, which I pass on to you.

One: Be open to God's leading. Seek it. Wait for it to be revealed in a thousand-and-one everyday ways—through reading, friends, encounters, circumstances, and prayer.

Two: In the meantime, complete the task at hand. Fulfill the present course which may yet prove useful in a way you cannot comprehend at the moment, and guidance will come to you on the road.

If you are convinced that life is meant to be ultimately more than meaningless, although full of human knowledge; if you are convinced that life is meant to be more than a pleasure-centered, egocentric existence that denies any final authority other than self-will; then you are ready for God's transformation—dying to self and living to Christ.

And it will come as you are open to Him—a redirected life for Him to use as a blessing to others. That, friend, is the God effect.

ETERNAL GOD, who has sought us from the first of time and will love us to the last, be with us in this hour to give us the guidance we seek. Help us ever to wait on you with patience, to do the task that comes to hand, confident in the knowledge that yours is the initiative, yours is the power to change, and that the outcome is in your hands. So bless us through Christ. AMEN.

3

The God we adore

The Great Debate

A certain question has vexed countless minds for centuries: If God is all-powerful and all-good, why does evil exist?

One answer is to doubt God's power but not His goodness. Rabbi Harold Kushner, author of the best-seller *When Bad Things Happen to Good People*, writes, "I can worship a God who hates suffering but cannot eliminate it, more easily than I can worship a God who chooses to make children suffer and die." But are these the only alternatives?

A second solution does not doubt God's power but His goodness. A Holocaust survivor blames God for permitting six million Jewish deaths under the Nazis. "How can God redeem Himself?" he asks. "I don't know. I suppose He cannot." Another philosopher who acknowledges God's power but not His goodness contends that believers should protest for human justice and compassion thereby atoning for divine injustice. This attitude ends in worshipers who are better than the God they worship. Sophocles' complaint, "When gods do ill, why should we worship them?" thus has great cogency.

In this great debate, are the only alternatives to believe in a God who is loving but pathetically inadequate, or a God of power who simply does not care? Neither entity is worthy of our worship.

*
**

We Christians believe, as John states in 1 John 4:16, that God is Love. But, as I have said before, it all depends what you mean by "God." And most assuredly, it also depends what you mean by "Love." For many people the phrase "God is Love" is the maximum of ambiguity and absurdity in the minimum of words. Such a statement, unexplained, which blindly ignores the kind of world in which we live is more likely to lead thinking people to discard God than to reverence Him.

The world is full of hungry, homeless, wandering, unhappy people, full of contradiction in which the good and the grim exist side by side. It does not appear to be the protégé of a loving, powerful God. We think of the wickedness in men and women expressed in murder, war, slavery, torture, persecution, and the gas chamber. Civilization often seems to be a thin veneer covering something inherently worse than just the nature of the beast. Yet, while mankind's evil produces great pain and horror, it is perhaps less perplexing than the other grimness that seems to leap out from the very scheme of things.

In nature, completely free from man's intervention, we still find suffering and fear, cries of pain not praise—for instance from the little birds, victims of the butcherbird or shrike who impales them alive on thorns and eats them later. Ornithologists tell us that the robin's song is not a paean of praise to the Creator, but a vocal warning to other birds that this is his territory and he will fight for it if necessary.

An irreverent limerick makes a valid point against all

shallow thinkers who would glibly speak of God's goodness as self-evident:

> There was a young lady of Ryde
> Who was carried away by the tide.
> A man-eating shark
> Was heard to remark,
> "I knew that the Lord would provide."

We have to admit that we live in a world where one species of fish or animal feeds upon another in an atmosphere of fear and hostility; a world of viruses, germs, earthquakes, hurricanes, famines, and floods. All living matter is subject to disease. Nothing is exempt. Everything would seem to be poisoned almost at the source.

Life is obviously a desperately serious business. We can see that others who differ from us in their conclusions about God have certain grounds. It is no wonder that a philosopher like John Stuart Mill said in the last century that God was either good, but not powerful; or He was powerful, but not good. Here we have the old accusation against God for His tolerance of evil. If God is Love, they argue, He could not let mankind suffer in agony unless He were powerless to prevent it; if He were powerful enough to prevent it, He could not be Love to allow it. This naturally leads many to discard God entirely, for how can we worship One who is less kind than ourselves? Or loving, but quite inadequate?

Consider the position in which those who feel this way are now left. They have disposed of the problem of evil by denying that it is of any significant meaning and accepting that it is the less pleasant side of the way things happen to be. Once they deny that there is a purposive Power, Mind, Being, and Creator behind the universe, obviously everything just "happened" by sheerest accident. What we call "evil" in mankind is therefore reduced to the level of growing pains, vestiges of his primeval fight for survival that may well be eradicated by increased enlightenment and self-knowledge. This we have yet to see.

The real problem for those who thus dispose of God is that they now have to explain good. Where did "good"—as revealed in a love of truth, justice, beauty, healing and compassion, unselfishness, and humility—come from? Such qualities have been the highest mark of human development worldwide through the centuries. If these also are the product of accident (as they must be according to this view) why should they be regarded as better than lies, injustice, ugliness, destruction, selfishness, and hate? We could understand if it were more pleasant and self-regarding for men and women to seek the good, but the usual fate of those who have sought it has been at best, misunderstanding, and at worst, martyrdom.

Many fine humanists seek and value the good. Why? For the sake of others? For the sake of the race? Again, why? If all life is a purposeless accident going nowhere at the end of the day—why? They claim to seek the good for their day and age without prejudice and with true zeal for human brotherhood and sisterhood. How noble! Yet how ungracious to crave the true but then logically have to deny that it has any source other than their own "accidentally created" minds. To revere the goodness in mankind while rejecting a God of goodness is like praising the play *Hamlet* while denying Shakespeare.

My contention is that while the Christian cannot have a cut-and-dried, irrefutable, here-and-now answer to the problem of evil in the world, the Christian has clues from the way God in Christ deals with evil. Clues that there is a solution—a solution more true to the realities of good and evil than the humanistic denial of the existence of a loving God which reduces evil to "just one of those things" and goodness to a stream without a source which will eventually peter out in the sands of time. A solution, moreover, that does not end up with the worship of an indifferent Almighty or a loving inadequate.

*
**

What then is God's way of dealing with evil, and remaining consistent with His being both loving and powerful? It is a twofold attack.

First, despite all appearances to the contrary, God demonstrates His Love. He does this by entering the setup Himself, by experiencing firsthand through Jesus the malignancy of human sin which is more potent than many people seem to realize. Sin will not be defeated by mere benevolence. Good intentions in the head are no more effective against sin than flowers in the hair. A soft tolerance—"If you won't bother me, Jack, I won't bother you"—cuts no ice against hatred and viciousness, prejudice and pride, selfishness and greed. To incant "All you need is Love," ad nauseam, will not alter the real situation of evil one whit. It all depends what you mean by Love.

When we Christians say that God is Love, we mean that God in Christ tackled sin and bore its full brunt. Injustice, malice, betrayal and beating, denial and despair, forsakenness and desolation, jealousy and envy, taunting and mockery, rejection and condemnation fell upon Him. And He took it, for our sake. It is all very well for those who don't want to make very much of sin to talk glibly of a gentle, kind, beneficent attitude as being sufficient to put mankind right, and call this shallow, wishy-washy thing "Love." Those who have experienced for themselves something of the insidiousness, the resilience, the scope, and the depth of evil know that no Love can be said to have borne it that has not faced evil at its worst, plumbed its depths and

challenged its power with sheer goodness, not mere genial-
ity or good intentions. Only One has done this—Jesus
Christ.

Whatever else the Cross shows, it reveals two things
unmistakably. One is the basic evil in humanity. For Jesus
was done to death not by peculiarly bad people, criminal
types, but by "decent" people who knew better. It is ever
the way, for sin is no respecter of persons or status. The
Cross also declares the Love of God, which challenges this
evil with goodness. "Forgive them," cries the Sinless One
as He hangs there. Even in the face of death's victory and
with a sense of utter aloneness upon Him, Jesus' words are,
"Father, into Thy hands I trust my Spirit."

No one can go further for another in love than God in
Christ has gone for us. That is the first prong of God's way
of dealing with evil: He bears it and thereby shows His
Love. The world can never again be an utterly tragic,
desolate, God-forsaken place. The Cross shows that God
has not forsaken it or us, then or now.

*
**

The second part of God's twofold attack on evil is to
work through it and achieve His end despite it. This is
where we see God's power. Many people think they would
know how to use godlike powers. They would put down
dictators, stop wars, eliminate disease, prevent crime, do
away with drugs, save the environment, and so on. Now, if
God really has power, why doesn't He do this? Why doesn't
He act like a good person?

It is here that we have to ask what God's purpose is in
the whole human setup. The Bible is the record of His
revelation to men and women and it tells us that God made
us for fellowship with Himself. This is His purpose. We are
neither robots nor puppets. We are beings with choice, free

to love or to hate, to accept or reject Him. But this end does not justify the use of any means. The end determines what the means are to be. For example, a teacher with a large and difficult class could no doubt get on splendidly by excluding the lazy, the backward, and the disobedient. But then her purpose would be strictly limited to the education of the bright and the biddable. Yet her purpose is to teach them all and this she can do only at the cost of keeping them all in the class.

This world is full of God's children. That is what He wants us to be. Certainly, it would look impressive if He used His power dramatically in a draconian way to get rid of the bad. Yet it would really be an admission of weakness, for it would defeat His purpose of not being willing that any should perish, but that all might find life in Him. If people perish spiritually it will not be because He has shut them out, but because they have rejected Him.

God's power is to be seen in His ability to achieve His purpose despite everything that stands against His will and everything that seems God-denying, despite all allegations that if He is good, He is powerless. He is not powerless. His purpose, to bring us all to Himself, determines the use of His power. He uses it in the face of evil to work good with those who cooperate with Him.

The Resurrection of Christ is the unmistakable guarantee of this. Here was mankind's representative who cooperated fully. From that first Easter morning, the worst that sin could do at Calvary was transformed into the best that God has done. The grave became an empty tomb, the tragedy a triumph. Sinners who believed in Him were now sons and daughters who lived new lives. History had a goal and this Cross was the signpost.

For twenty centuries men and women worldwide who have staked their lives on God's Love have known the power

of Christ's Presence. With one accord they would state with
John:

> God is Love, and His Love was disclosed to us in this:
> that He sent His only Son into the world to bring us
> life. The Love we speak of is not our love for God, but
> the Love He showed to us.

Friend, that vision can do for us what nothing else ever
can. It can give us a new life now, as we accept God's
purpose for us and experience His Loving Power in us to
see it through—the ultimate answer in the great debate,
this side of death. This is the God we adore. Loving.
Powerful. Present.

HOLY LORD, who revealed yourself in all humility and
weakness in the child in the manger, therein is your power
brought low. Your power is also brought low in the Cross
of Christ, yet we can barely realize such Love as is shown
there. Help us now to see your Love: caring for us, revealing yourself, bearing our sins, taking them away, undergo-
ing the maximum that we have to face. Help us to see your
Power saving us: despite our sin, despite our wrong-head-
edness and self-will, despite the evil we bring upon ourselves and do to others. Lord, grant us a new vision of your
sacrifice to see that you are Loving Power and Powerful
Love combined and present in Jesus our Savior. This we ask
in His name. AMEN.

4

How do you "see" God?

The Undetected God

My text today is from the Book of Job 9:11:

Were He to pass me I should not see Him, nor detect His stealthy movement.

Poor Job is in a quandary. He is a man of honor and integrity who has undergone some ghastly experiences—property loss, large-scale family bereavement, and personal ill-health. His so-called friends maintain that as God does not afflict the innocent, Job's suffering must be the result of some hidden sin he has committed. Job denies this vehemently, still trusting in the Creator who apparently lets this happen, saying in effect:

If only I could put my case to Him. Could there be some kind of approach between us? But how can this be? He is the Creator and I am the creature. Who will be the go-between? Where is the point of contact? I am mortal. He is infinite. Were He to pass me I should not see Him, nor detect His stealthy movement.

The Undetected God.

To see God is the most tenacious of the spiritual hopes of humanity. In every age, in every part of the world, there have been those inherent mystics who have sought a vision of God for themselves. In a way, this can be a selfish desire to have a unique monopoly on God. The possessor of such an experience would obviously be one of the spiritual elite. But the Bible does not encourage that sort of vision. The Bible's main stress is upon the Word which, being heard, calls for obedience, and from the obedience comes the seeing. But what kind of "seeing" is this anyway? How do you "see" God?

*
**

There is the literalistic approach to seeing, which many take as being only a physical matter. This can be illustrated by the philosophers' parable of two explorers who came across a clearing in the jungle where both flowers and weeds were growing. One said, "Some gardener must tend this spot." The other disagreed. They pitched their tents and set a watch but no one appeared. The first said, "Perhaps the gardener is invisible." So they put up a barbed wire fence, electrified it, and patrolled it with bloodhounds. Yet there was no movement, no shout, and the bloodhounds gave no cry. The believer is still not convinced and insists, "There is a gardener—invisible, intangible, and insensible to shock who has no scent and makes no sound, yet comes secretly to look after the garden he loves." The skeptic replies, "But how does what you call an invisible, intangible, eternally elusive gardener differ from an imaginary gardener or even no gardener at all?"

Put "God" in the place of the "gardener." The skeptic's implication is that God is qualified out of existence because He cannot be perceived by sensory tests and materialistic methods, and therefore, whoever believes in the existence of such a God on whom there can be no check is a sentimental, gullible fool. But is this true? Has the believer absolutely no checks?

Our physical means of perception, the five senses, matter. But within the animal kingdom, we know that we are in some ways inferior to other creatures. We do not see as keenly as the eagle, have the dog's sense of smell, or the acute hearing of the red deer, and so on. Yet while some of our senses are inferior to those of animals, we have a faculty denied them—the ability to think creatively, to reason, form concepts, hold ideals, envisage great purposes and goals, be elevated by beauty which the eye of the eagle may see more clearly but never appreciates, be moved by words the red deer could hear from a far greater distance but never understand. This is simply to say that humans are more than animals and can grasp deeper truths than can be conveyed by sight, sound, and smell alone.

It is through this uniquely human awareness that we reach beyond the message of physical senses to grasp the force of the moral imperative "ought" along with insight into words like justice, freedom, duty, truth, and love. It is through the proper development and "tuning," as it were, of this nonmaterial sense, that we perceive God individually, and we "see." The poet declares:

> Chief of all God's wondrous works,
>   Supreme of all His Plan,
> He has put an upward reach
>   In the heart of Man.

We all have this "upward reach" latent within us. But like many other faculties, it is often neglected and left unexercised and dormant until it finally dies. This is what Jesus stresses when He quotes Isaiah to the people:

You will hear and hear, but never understand; you will
look and look, but never see; for this people has grown
gross at heart. Their ears are dull. Their eyes are closed.
Otherwise, their eyes might see, their ears hear, their
heart understand, and then they might turn again and
I might heal them.

There's more to seeing than meets the eye. Unless we
develop this "more," we shall be blind to the meaning of
our lives on earth and God will pass by undetected. "Were
He to pass me," says Job, "I should not see Him, nor detect
His stealthy movement." And this is true. For the Creator
God is beyond the five senses and cannot be discerned as
an infinite projection of material mankind.

*
**

What prevents us from seeing God spiritually? In a way,
the same thing that makes us fail to see people in the
street—a complete preoccupation with something else.

Was there ever a time when in popular writing and on
television more stress was laid upon the physical and animal
heritage of people? Here we are—naked apes running
around the human zoo. One might be forgiven for thinking
that this is all there is to humankind—animal antics. People-
watchers never see God, if people are all they're watching.
Again, the current commercialization of sex is another
preoccupation that devalues human relations, dehumanizes
the human share in creation, and takes up the attention of
millions. Even in the ordinary run of things, the material
comes first. People concentrate on their houses, their cars,
their entertainment, their food, their clothes, their work,
their leisure, their bankbooks, their stocks and shares, their
vacations. If that's what they are doing, how impossible it

is for them to "see" God. Their minds are preoccupied with their own priorities.

When people are totally absorbed with themselves and reckon the real meaning of life only in terms of the material, it is no wonder that God becomes invisible to them and they become incapable of "seeing" Him. Having reached supposed "maturity," they dismiss God as an outmoded creation of their own infancy or fancy. But make no mistake. We can only dismiss the gods we have created. The God who created us will not be dismissed and remains the source of ultimate meaning.

There is the story of a preoccupied professor in Edinburgh who met a student while crossing the North Bridge which runs from the university down to Princes Street above Waverley Station. They talked for a while until on parting the professor looked up the road and asked, "By the way, was I coming in that direction when we met?" "No sir," the student replied. "Ah!" said the professor, "then I will have had my lunch!"

I would seriously suggest that mankind is so preoccupied that it really doesn't know whether it's coming or going. Seeking meaning in all the lesser things, much of humanity is taken up with that which does not ultimately satisfy, and has little or no awareness left of One who made us for fellowship with Himself, a relationship which transforms our transient life into something of eternal significance.

*
**

But how do we see God? If we admit we often have a preoccupation elsewhere which prevents us from grasping spiritual truth, is it then only a matter of concentrating less on material things that would allow us to detect Him? No, not quite. There is a definite prerequisite for seeing God. I said earlier that the Bible does not encourage any selfish desires to see God that mankind may have—any vision that could be a claim to spiritual superiority.

In the Old Testament, there are only a handful of instances (Moses, Isaiah, and Ezekiel for example) where man has a vision of God. But in no case were those men seeking it for its own sake. It was by God's initiative in the life of each. Such a vision was not the goal of their lives but the point of departure from which they moved on to accomplish God's purpose. These few apart, it is the general principle of the Old Testament that no one can see God. Not just because He is invisible, but because He is essentially holy.

There are two sides to this holiness of God. On the one hand, it means that He is completely other than human—the separate, unanalyzable, unfathomable Creator. On the other hand, God's holiness confronts mankind in a dynamic and exacting way, offering men and women new life through a relationship with His Being. This is precisely what the Old Covenant is all about—the relationship of sinful people to God's holiness.

In Psalm 24, these two aspects are found side by side.

> The earth is the Lord's, and the fullness thereof;
> The world, and they that dwell therein.
> For He hath founded it upon the seas,
> And established it upon the floods.

Here we have the Holy One—other than mankind and Creator of mankind. The psalm then goes on to speak of human sin confronted by this dynamic holiness:

> Who shall ascend into the hill of the Lord?
> Or who may stand in His holy place?

A good question. What are the qualifications for approaching God's presence, for seeing him? The psalm gives the answer: clean hands, pure hearts, and no falseness within. Such are the prerequisites. This has nothing to do with our eyesight, but a lot to do with our egos.

"Blessed," says Christ, "happy are the pure in heart, for they shall see God." Pure in heart—the whole personality involving will, mind, and emotions—is a character qualification, not a university degree.

We know that there are people who can look at any situation, no matter how wholesome, and find in it material for their double meanings and their soiled sneers. In complete contrast is the happy person Jesus describes who looks out at all kinds of circumstances and people from a nature that is clear, single-minded, unprejudiced, and generous, who forever sees grace and guidance, goodness and God, everywhere.

Says John Keble:

> Thou who hast given us eyes to see
> And love this sight so fair,
> Give us a heart to find out Thee
> And read Thee everywhere.

Character qualification.

*
**

One last question: Where especially do we see God? There is no doubt about it—supremely in Jesus Christ. His claim is, "He that hath seen Me, hath seen the Father," and that claim has been confirmed by all who have had the character qualification to check it. But where do we see Christ today? The everyday Christ is seen in the life of the everyday Christian. And the everyday Christian is the person who detects Jesus in the ordinary people he or she meets day after day.

Tolstoy tells the story of the old shoemaker, Martin, a genuine Christian who is assured that Christ will come to visit him on a particular day. The cobbler makes the little workroom where he lives as clean and ready as he can. But his disappointment grows as the day wears on and he's only been visited by a child, a woman, and an old man. Night falls and there is still no sign of Christ. Then the truth dawns on him that in each one of these ordinary people who did call, to whom he gave the help they needed, Christ had indeed passed by. Where love is, God is.

Real Christians reveal Christ. They can do no other. When we come to the point of hearing Jesus' word, "Inasmuch as you did it for one of the least of these, you did it for Me," and live by it, we are very close to detecting the God who in Christ identified Himself with all mankind. And still does.

Our Christianity is a failure if God passes by in our neighbor and we do not detect Him. But if we do, we in our turn unconsciously become a visual aid to others who are seeking to detect Him for themselves. May we live in such a way that they can see the Christ in us.

> Thy face with reverence and with love,
> We in Thy children see,
> O may we minister to them
> And in them, Lord, to Thee.

This is how God is detected when He passes by. For there's so much more to "seeing" than meets the eye.

HEAVENLY FATHER, give us the eye of faith that we may perceive your presence in other people; that we may strive to stretch out our hands in love. As we do this, may we each one, unselfconsciously and unawares, become a person in whom others can see something of you. Through Christ we ask it. AMEN.

II

The Revelation of Jesus Christ

5

What Christ really did

Sin and the At-One-Ment

One of the cruelest things that can be done to people is to destroy the props that are helping them to live the Christian life day by day, and to put nothing of certainty in their place. It is justifiable only if the shake-up is designed to show more clearly that which cannot be shaken: the truth at the heart of the matter. Today I put before you one of the unshakable foundations.

Five times in the letters to Timothy there occurs this phrase, "Here are words you may trust." Each time it refers to something which the early Christians believed was of the essence of faith. Look first at 1 Timothy 1:15: "Here are words you may trust, words that merit full acceptance: Christ Jesus came into the world to save sinners." At this point I want us to fix our minds on what Christ came into the world to do—to save sinners, to be the Atonement.

Atonement is the official technical term for teaching about the life and death of Christ, and what he really did. The word was coined by the old translator of the Bible into English, William Tyndale. Struggling to find a word that would carry the full meaning of the Greek term Paul originally used to describe the redeeming work of Christ

(Romans 5:11), Tyndale invented this one by joining together two simpler words, "at" and "onement," making "atonement." This, then, is the work of Christ: to make "at one" God and mankind.

*
**

Over the centuries there have been various theories of the atonement and how it was accomplished. The trouble with such theories is not that they are untrue, but that they are inadequate. Inadequate because they don't go far enough. Indeed, in a sense no human view can go far enough. There is mystery here that no human mind can confidently penetrate and come back with a neat summation of God's purpose.

But there is another kind of inadequacy in these theories of atonement. Many revolve around a particular word picture, forgetting that no one analogy can express what Christ did in His life and death. For instance, what has been called the "satisfaction" theory (in which the death of Christ is somehow looked on as squaring the account on behalf of sinful mankind) hinges on a view of sin as being a failure to pay the debt we owe to God. Or, again, the "penal" theory stresses the punishment of sin as being the necessary amends that the honor and justice of God require, and Jesus is made the figure in the dock, substituting for us. Sin is the crime supreme. Then there are those who insist that the Cross really is the wonderful revelation of the Love of God, which it is. But that still leaves the unanswered question, why this particular way? Isn't sin more than just the dark backcloth that highlights the brightness of love?

You see, if some have pictured sin as a "debt," then obviously into their picture of the Atonement will come commercial elements of account squaring. If sin is viewed as "crime," a breach of law, then legal, judicial ideas are attached to God's way of redemption. Or if sin is regarded as the "human darkness," the blackness of the heart, the blindness of the mind, then the Cross is the searchlight piercing the night and showing it up by contrast.

There is, I believe, a very definite link between views of what sin is and subsequent theories about how God deals with it in the Atonement. Clearly, if we picture sin as a crime requiring a penalty, then we'll end up with the view of God as judge, punishing the Sinless One in our place that His justice may be preserved somehow. This is not a particularly helpful picture. If Jesus came to reveal supremely a parent-like, loving God, crime and punishment is not the definitive description of the situation. "Christ Jesus came into the world to save sinners." Yes! But what is the essence of the sin that afflicts us? A debt, a crime, a darkness—are these adequate pictures?

James VI of Scotland and I of England wrote "A Counterblast to Tobacco," in which he said, "This is a branch of the sin of drunkenness which is the root of all sins." If that were true, you can see how simple Atonement would be. There would be no need to set up a Cross, just invite people to sign an abstinence pledge! No wonder James was called "the wisest fool in Christendom."

I believe that it is as we realize what Christ saves us from that we shall also discover something of how He saves us from it.

*
**

Sin is separational. "The sin ye do by two and two, ye must pay for one by one," says Kipling. And George Bernard Shaw writes:

> The worst sin towards our fellow-creatures is not to hate them, but to be indifferent to them: that's the essence of inhumanity.

There is no evading the fact that sin isolates. It cuts off concern. It produces suspicion. It doubts the loving hand, and it ignores whatever it chooses.

On the visible level, sin breaks and destroys the noblest friendships, the bond between the truest lovers, the best fellowship of the family. And on the invisible level, it produces a sense of estrangement, the consciousness of guilt, a certain inability to be at ease in the presence of the wronged person, even the feeling of being out of joint with life. "I wonder what's wrong with me?"—this "dis-ease," this shrugged-off alienation is at the core of sin.

Paul, in Romans 1, speaks of the human condition, of men who "boast of their wisdom but . . . have made fools of themselves, exchanging the splendor of immortal God for an image shaped like mortal man." And again:

> . . . knowing God, they have refused to honor him as God. . . . Hence all their thinking has ended in futility, and their misguided minds are plunged in darkness. . . . For this reason God has given them up to the vileness of their own desires . . . because they have bartered away the truth of God for the lie and have offered reverence and worship to created things instead of to the Creator.

There is the tragedy of the human situation. Sinful mankind has lost the knowledge of the God against whom they have sinned. They have made other gods with their own hands. They have set themselves up as god and they don't know why it's not working.

With their sins, men and women have built their own prisons. The windows are beyond the prisoners' reach. The sunlit world is a dream. They have forgotten what they were meant to be. This is the punishment sinners by themselves can never escape. They cannot repent because they do not know the One whom they have really offended. They are, deep down, alienated from their Creator. The separational effect of sin is its own dread punishment. Here we fail as human beings, and become God's fractured family.

Take this simple picture. You've seen the children's game on television in which competitors stand at one end of a teeter-totter, walk up it, over the pivot, and place building blocks one at a time at the other end. The hard part is to keep the positioned blocks in place when the seesaw tilts back. Now imagine a wee boy trying to do this without realizing that it was he himself who upset the blocks as he stumped back for the next one. All efforts end in frustration and tears. Then his father says, "I'll do it for you." And with perfect balance he takes his place on the pivot, realizing what is involved.

Let that be a parable of humanity, so unaware, so misunderstanding the balance of life that it constantly frustrates itself, until the Father says, "I'll do it for you." The Incarnation of Christ is the perfect balance of the human and the divine on which our destiny pivots.

"Equal with God," cries Paul, "but having become man, he humbled Himself." The Incarnation is the beginning of the end of mankind's alienation. For in all Christ did, there "did combine His human nature and His part divine." In Jesus we see both the human we were meant to be and the God we sin against. "Here are words you may trust. . . . Christ Jesus came into the world to save sinners; of whom I am chief," declares Paul.

*
**

Sin is separational, but moreover, sin is personal. Our divided, disorderly, self-assertive world reflects division, disorder, and aggression in the self of each person. Says John Donne:

> Wilt Thou forgive that sin where I begun,
> Which is my sin, though it were done before?

There is a personal element about sin that makes a blanket deal about debts or an all-inclusive punishment awarded to One, an inappropriate description of God's way of dealing with something so intimate, so insidious, so second nature to each individual.

The Passion of Christ is equally personal. He who humbled Himself and became obedient to the point of accepting the death of the Cross did so for this reason—that each man and woman might be reconciled to God. Reconciliation is ever a personal thing involving forgiveness offered and received. Charles Wesley describes it:

> Died He for me, who caused His pain—
> For me, who Him to death pursued?
> Amazing love! how can it be
> That Thou, my God, shouldst die for me?

The Cross reveals both God's offer and also what it cost God in Christ to make that offer personally. There is, as the poet says:

> . . . no expeditious road
> To pack and label folk for God
> And save them by the barrel-load.

Atonement is not a negotiated settlement on behalf of all union members. So the old question put by the Negro spiritual is true, "Were you there when they crucified my Lord?" Until we recognize our part *in* that Cross, there is no reconciliation for us *through* that Cross.

*
**

Sin is separational. It takes the Incarnation to end the alienation. Sin is personal. It takes the sacrifice of the only begotten Son to reconcile each sinner to the Father. And sin is ultimately spiritual. Burns notes in his "Epistle to a Young Friend":

> I waive the quantum o' the sin,
>   The hazard of concealing;
> But, och! it hardens a' within,
>   And petrifies the feeling!

Individual sins are but the tip of the iceberg of spiritual deadness. So we must come to life spiritually before we can fully understand the Atonement; otherwise, it is only a word. If we want to understand God's reconciliation of the world to Himself, we listen to those who have known it as a reality in themselves. If we ask them, "How do you know that the one Christ died for all?" they only answer, "At any rate, He died for me!" If we ask, "How do you know that?" they will say with Paul that they somehow experience "a share in His sufferings and in the power of His Resurrection." This experience is beyond words, for words are rigid and the Spirit is life. And what they mean by "somehow" is the ongoing work of the Holy Spirit. The Atonement is made real to every believer only by the Presence of Christ within him or her through the Spirit.

The Atonement is not only deliverance from sin. It is our growth to righteousness in the Spirit, our share in the new order. It is recognition that beyond the Incarnation, beyond the Resurrection, Jesus Christ is the name above every name, the Lord to whom every knee shall bow—the only One who can save sinners—you and me—from the sin that is separational, personal, and spiritual.

> He breaks the power of canceled sin,
>   He sets the prisoner free;

His blood can make the foulest clean,
His blood availed for me.

"Here are words you may trust."

MOST GRACIOUS GOD, with grateful hearts we focus on your Christ, who for our sakes became Man, endured the Cross, despising the shame; who has opened up the way to life assuring us that death is only sleep. May we, in simple trust, live in your light, order our paths by your truth and righteousness, and rejoice every day in gladness since we are more than conquerors through Him that loved us. In His name. AMEN.

6

The testing time

Do Something!

What can we do to achieve peace and justice in our world? That question has constantly presented itself to all people of humanity and goodwill, but never more so than now. Through the technologies of our time, the instant media brings strife, famine, injustice, and suffering right into our living rooms day after day—something which never happened at the start of this century. We are far removed in quantity, if not in content, from those early days of telegraph when the report on a bygone Prince of Wales convalescing after appendicitis was described:

> Swift o'er the wire, the electric message came,
> "He is not better. He is much the same."

Things today are *not* much the same. Ordinary people have an enormous quantity of information. They are aware of international tensions, conflicts near and far, catastrophes as they happen, economic inequities, and myriad points of view in comment. So what do they do?

In the last decade various attempts at peace have been made: an American schoolgirl writes to the Russian leader;

men and women here and in Europe march, protest, lie down, and stand up against nuclear weapons deployment; a stubborn man threatens to blow up the Washington Monument so that the world may be forced into peaceful ways, and dies in his bluff. I'm not suggesting that these illustrations all fall into the same category, but they certainly show how ordinary people try to do something toward what seems to be a good end—peace.

By the fall of 1989 we were seeing a tremendous relaxing of international tensions, a new growth of freedom in many societies formerly oppressed for decades by dead dogma. This is genuine cause for rejoicing. Yet we must beware the temptation to think that peace, freedom, and the ability to make different economic choices are, once achieved, the ultimate goals of life. After all, the most self-centered hedonist is all for peace lest his lifestyle be affected. Peace can provide greater freedom to make choices. But if the choice is wrong, people end up not with liberty but enslaved by license. Almost everyone wants outward peace, yet it does not follow that each individual wants to walk that inward path which alone leads to true peace.

The Bible tells us that God in Christ is our peace, both personal and pervasive. Apart from that life-changing relationship to God which produces people who are no longer self-willed but God-controlled in everything they do, the best human efforts are ultimately futile. Natural unredeemed humanity does not wish to know this. People tend to think that if only they had the power, they could change things for the better. But it doesn't always work that way.

"All right," says someone. "What about the Church giving a lead? Doing something!"

"Amen," I would agree, depending on two things: what you mean by "Church" and what you mean by "lead."

*
**

The Church, to me, means the whole body of Christians committed to Christ living in the every day of the twentieth century: heirs to the faith once delivered to the saints; possessors of the promise; the leaven in the lump of society; loving fellow-workers with Christ. These make up the current Church on earth, though clerics, courts and councils, popes and prelates may have their place.

And what is the "lead" the Church has to give? In the early eighties, I was sent a study-paper called "Christian Faith and Economic Justice" for my comment. It laid considerable stress on the sinful structures and systems in society. On one of the pages it stated:

> Structural changes cannot achieve all that is necessary for human wholeness and community, but they can provide greater justice in society.

I found myself asking, "Is this the Church's primary business, of equal importance with the Gospel?" I had my answer when the 1989 General Assembly of the Presbyterian Church (USA) voted to elevate "doing justice" to one of the Church's two top priorities for the remainder of the century. This goal is ranked equally with the denomination's other number one priority—"doing evangelism."

They are not equal. I realize, of course, that committed Christians have a tremendous effect on the structures of society. They've had a tremendous effect over the centuries. But this effect has been a result of the changes in their own lives. The faith produces the works. And that is the order.

I feel that over some decades the social gospel has become an alternative to the Good News rather than its outcome. This alternative is attractive because of visible, outward results: a sense of moving and shaking; a desire to be where it looks as though the real action is. The Good News, however, remains the same old slow business of sowing seed in the often intractable ground of human nature, and hopefully leaving the harvest to God.

I am not suggesting for one moment that Christians should not be intelligently and energetically involved in bringing Christian views to bear on society's structures and resulting problems, political and socioeconomic. Of course they should—acting appropriately on their own insights, expertise, positions, and talents. By our Christian faithfulness or lack of it in these matters, we shall be judged. This is the lead that the Church through all its members must give.

Nonetheless, the Church per se should not be in the business of simply pointing at this or that system as the villain of the piece. Christ went after souls not systems, for it is people who make systems work for weal or woe. Could there have been a more brutal system than the Roman Empire built on slavery, force, and inequity for the poor? Why did Christ not go for the system? Because He knew well that changing systems is a futile business without changing people.

The Church is primarily called to proclaim by word and deed the Good News of Christ who alone changes human nature. When we think we know better than that, we are in danger of yielding to the temptation of power.

*
**

I began with the question, "What can we do to achieve peace and justice in our world?" But should that really be the primary question for Christians? For surely peace is something deeper than the mere absence of armed aggression; God's justice is more than any economic leveling can achieve. If this is so, as I am sure it is, we must beware of confusing the normal desire for human preservation with the peace which God wants for each one of us; and equally, of confusing any vaunted politico-economic structure with the advent of the Kingdom of God and His righteousness on earth.

If we are seeking a lesser peace and righteousness, we shall be tempted into thinking that to achieve it all we need is some kind of power. When will we learn that the path of power is the most deceptive and corrupting way in the world? Deceptive because power tempts its users with what often appears a quick and easy, if dubious, means to a desired end; corrupting because the people who seek it are rarely, if ever, good enough in themselves in the first place to be able to handle it without yielding to its insidious ego-expanding effects.

The Christian's aim must always be the same as Christ's: to seek and to do God's will which alone produces true peace and justice. How do we go about it? For guidance, see the way Jesus took in answer to that question. Look at the forty days Christ spent in the wilderness: He was led—and tempted. Matthew 4:1:

> Then was Jesus led up by the Spirit into the wilderness to be tempted by the devil.

"Led by the Spirit . . . tempted by the devil." This is a fair and apt description of the position of the Church and the individual Christian in the wilderness of today's world.

Immediately after the great spiritual experience of divine commissioning at His baptism, Jesus is put to the test. The question for Him—and for us—is still the same. We, too, are commissioned and led by the Spirit, seeking to do God's will. But how? Do something! But what? This is where the temptation strikes.

*
**

"If Thou be the Son of God, command that these stones be made bread," whispers the tempting voice.

Jesus in the wilderness is hungry. He has not eaten for a long time. All around Him are stones, looking for all the world like little loaves. "Is this the way?" He wonders. "People are hungry. Human need is all too evident. Roman taxes grind down the poor. There's a desperate struggle just to stay alive. Surely it is right and fair to overturn the social injustice—to make stones bread on a large scale? Will not the Kingdom of God come this way?"

Christ's own compassion and the world's obvious inequity give this temptation tremendous force. But it must be resisted. Mankind does live by bread, and economic justice is part of the Christian's concern. But mankind does not live by bread alone. There is a spiritual appetite, a God-given food. Jesus has come to do God's will which is not just to satisfy segments of society materially, but to save a whole world spiritually and forever.

Twenty years ago I heard David Sheppard, Bishop of Liverpool and a professional cricketer, speak about liberation theology. He kept stressing what seemed to be God's special main concern: the impoverished and the oppressed. Afterwards I said to an older minister, "That's not right. He's bowling us a googly." (You can imagine what a googly is—full of spin and bias.) We agreed that it was almost as if the Good News Christ proclaimed was no more than an economic bonanza. For no attempt was made to distinguish between the materially poor (who, along with the rich, certainly have the Gospel preached to them) and "the poor in spirit" who, irrespective of their material status, are the ones who admit their need of God and who are the possessors of the Kingdom of Heaven.

It may be that those who lack the buffer of wealth and privilege turn more readily to God for help, but not necessarily. The fact is that whether we are rich or poor, we shall

all be judged by our response to God in what we did with what we had. The New Testament economic theme is a right stewardship, not a call for revolution, socialist leveling, or entrepreneurial capitalism. The equality we must strive toward for Christian justice is an equality of caring because God cares equally for all and wants the fellowship of each one. We cannot enter into this fellowship without having God's attitude of equal care for all His family, not just segments. Jesus says, "God sends His sunshine and rain on the just and the unjust"—the good and bad alike. We are to emulate our Heavenly Father in showing an all-embracing love that does not play favorites. The New Testament tells us that "God is no respecter of persons"—rich or poor.

Robin Hood has always been a popular folk hero. To take from the rich and give to the poor may well reduce material inequity. However, even if we had the power to do it, this would not necessarily make better people of either the rich or the poor. God's purpose is new creatures and changed lives. This can only be effected by the Spirit of Christ, not the spirit of Robin Hood.

Think of the incident where a certain village would not receive Jesus and His disciples. The disciples want Him to call down fire from heaven to obliterate the people. He rebukes them saying, "You know not what manner of spirit you are of." Scholars say the origin of this verse is doubtful. But there is nothing doubtful about the fact that it reflects the mind of Christ made abundantly clear elsewhere: namely, that a desire for power and the wrong spirit do not combine to work the works of God. For the Christ who would not snuff out the smoldering wick or break the bruised reed is come to save the world. And that takes all the power of love, not all the love of power.

To satisfy materially is open to the power that can make stones bread and make the desert blossom as the rose—which we now have the technological power to do. But it is

not enough. We are still more than body. To satisfy spiritually, to nourish souls, is no quick business but the slow,
difficult process of quickening a lethargic appetite: awakening unrealized taste; prompting a deep craving; meeting a
hidden hunger even in those fed, clothed, and materially
well-off. This is the Church's primary task in the world, and
from this work all the rest flows.

*
**

It is not possible to cover the temptation of Christ in one
sermon, and I shall continue this theme in the next two.
But let me complete this opening portion on the first
temptation and the question still before us. How do we do
God's will?

We must not simply equate this with every self-preserving
desire for peace; the peace God gives is more than physical
safety. Nor must we identify economic reallocation with the
coming of the Kingdom; mankind does not live by bread
alone. Any clear reading of the Gospel shows that God
sends His Son not just to a world of wars here and there,
or of poverty here and there, but to a whole world lost in
its inmost being everywhere. Aggression, hatred, fear, oppression, and misery are but the symptoms; alienation from
God, the cause. Lostness is the human condition for which
Christ sacrifices Himself. That condition cuts across economic, political, and every other stratum, requiring not
bread, but the Cross to rectify.

Henri Nouwen, in his book *The Wounded Healer,* says:

> Changing the human heart and changing human soci-
> ety are not separate tasks, but are as interconnected as
> the two beams of the Cross.

Yes, but take that analogy one step further.
Never forget that the cross beam, the transverse beam

which reaches out horizontally into society and all our dealings and relationships there, depends for its whole support on the perpendicular beam of each Christian's personal relationship to God. Without that support, it simply does not stay up.

What we can accomplish of God's will in the world depends entirely on how much we have allowed God in Christ to accomplish His will in us. Again and again, the choice is: Love of power—the temptation; or power of Love—the Spirit's leading.

ETERNAL LORD, grant us your grace that in our own lives we may be changed by you. Thus may we affect the lives of those around us and the world in which we live. Help us to realize that we must follow Christ here, as everywhere; be led of Him by His Spirit and be able to see the clear way before us. In His name we ask it. AMEN.

7

Playing the world's game?

Temptations to Power

On Thin Ice is the title of a book brought out not long ago by Roy Howard Beck, a top-notch religion reporter. His story concerns what should have been his innocent years at the *United Methodist Reporter* covering Protestant Church news. It shows how an honest, liberal reporter discovered to his astonishment and moral dismay the way manipulative, far-left staffers in the mainline Churches had been making use of those Churches. He gives many illustrations. Here is one.

He was asked to examine the human rights record of the National Council of Churches, and noted that both Freedom House and Amnesty International found that the thirty-six nations with the worst human rights records were almost evenly split between right-wing and left-wing governments. He expected to find a similar evenly divided set of actions by the National Council of Churches. But no. Eighty percent of the Council's human rights actions were taken in response to abuses committed by right-wing governments. The Council's explanation of this admitted tilt was that the U.S. government had more clout with right-wing governments and the United States itself was sometimes supportive of the repression: thus the Council focused its criticism and pressure where it could achieve the most results—on its own government and allies. "The tilt," writes Mr. Beck, "made the Churches' human rights work appear at times to be more of a political movement than a fulfillment of Christian ministry."

This double standard is evident elsewhere. An official of the World Council of Churches indicated that criticism of the Soviet Union would bring reprisals against the Russian Orthodox Church, whereas Churches in democratic nations face no such hazards. Indeed one Russian Orthodox representative said that his delegation would withdraw from the Council if any resolution critical of Soviet policy were passed. So it was not passed. One of the World Council staffers said, "The bottom line is: Who has the most to lose? The Russians." Not really. The World Council loses credibility by making judgments based on expediency rather than principle. Either apply the same standards to all, or do not pass judgment.

*
**

I mention this matter to bring into focus the theme I began earlier: Temptations to Power—playing the world's game. These temptations arise as we ask the question, "How do we do God's will in the world?"

I have pointed out that it is a mistake simply to equate God's will with a human desire for peace and economic justice. God's will does indeed produce a true peace, but it is one centered on each individual's personal relationship to Him, not some lowest common denominator of self-preservation. Moreover, His justice is more than any economic theory or system can achieve. It finds expression in right stewardship. Ultimately, God judges each one of us—rich or poor—by what we do with what we now have. A forced leveling of income does not achieve His purpose, which is to save the whole world, not simply satisfy segments materially.

If we are seeking a lesser peace and justice, we will be tempted to think that all we need to achieve it is power. So instead of concentrating on quality proclamation of the unique Gospel which can make disciples of all nations and increase the quietly influential leaven in the lump of human society, the Church of today has often been drawn into promoting a social gospel as an alternative to the Good News rather than an outcome.

The more uncertain we are about the basics of our faith, the more tempted we are to associate with those forces in society that seem to be the movers and shakers. For their end appears to be good. They are helping people by economic justice. And surely if all the Christians in the world banded together in council, not only would they show the unity for which Christ prayed but they would also speak on important issues with a voice that would be heard. Sounds good.

But I fear that mixed in with all the good intent is a subtle yielding to the world's estimate of power: size, importance, and relevancy to the latest situation. The unity for which Christ prayed is a unity of the Spirit—the Spirit that recognizes fellow Christians by their relationship to Him, irrespective of background, color, or denomination. This basic unity certain Christians have always shown. It is not something that can be guaranteed by organizational means.

The enemy of the best is the second best. The danger which faces both the Church and individual Christians is like that confronting Christ when He is led by the Spirit into the wilderness to be tempted by the devil. It lies in the question, "How to do God's will?"

*
**

The first temptation is not an unworthy or evil answer. It is simply not sufficient. "Make stones bread! Tackle humanity's physical needs in a world of hunger and poverty."

Certainly, feeding the hungry and economic justice must be part of every Christian's right stewardship, for Christ's compassionate heart went out to those living in harshness and poverty under Roman rule. He knew the human evil which held power. He knew the tug of the social gospel before the phrase was ever coined. But He also knew that it was God's will to save the whole world, not just alleviate the misery of certain portions of it. That end determined the means He had to use.

God's human venture is with embodied souls, so mankind does not live by bread alone. There is an individual spiritual yearning to be satisfied, a hunger of the soul which no system, status, or sweetmeat can ever fill. Christ comes from God not primarily to save the world from war and injustice, but to save a world that is lost: people alienated from God, from their neighbor, and within themselves, a condition which exists even in the midst of peace and plenty. To declare this Good News is our prime task as Christians. From its individual, wholehearted acceptance by ordinary people must then flow the necessary lesser blessings.

This is a harder, slower road to take. If damning the system or meeting material need were all it took to save the world, then anyone with a love of power could have a go. But it takes more than that. It takes all the power of love, wide as the outstretched arms of the Cross that will not give in, give up, or let go of a single soul. This is the will of God that Jesus came to accomplish. The Church's chief commitment—and ours—is to the relevant declaration by lip and life, by every worthy means, of that reconciling work to the deepest needs of our world. To make something other than this the priority is to yield to the tempting shortcut of power's lesser means, which never achieves God's goal. Only the power of love can accomplish that.

"You have the power," says the tempter to Jesus. "Use it! Make these stones bread." And He had the power, else there would have been no temptation. He could have used it selfishly for His own hunger. He could have used it as a quick, easy way to gain a following. But Jesus resisted. He knew that the hunger He had come to meet could not be satisfied by bread or any other material thing, only by the love of God which He had come to show. The devil spoke true—He had the power—but it was the selfless power of Love. The Kingdom of God does not come without it. But for many it is too slow a way.

*
**

The second temptation came from a different angle. It was not, "You have the power—use it!" But, "God has the power. Test it. Jump!"

Perhaps you, like me, have put in time at the grocery checkout skimming through some of the papers which are ragbags of gossip, scandal, and astounding stuff. An article once caught my eye: two Italian researchers in Nepal had witnessed the monks of Lamaism. They quoted an Australian doctor who had spent years studying there. He had witnessed an incredible scene. "A monk—demonstrating his power for a degree in superior spirituality—called up rain and stopped it at will for four days in a row in a drought area, before a crowd of a hundred thousand people. I have no explanation for it. But that feat swept away all the skepticism I had."

My reaction is simply, "So what?" However outwardly dramatic, does such an event change the inward settled selfishness of the human spirit, renew broken personal relationships, or restore wounded souls? Of course not. It merely swells the chorus of those who reiterate Shakespeare's words in *Hamlet*:

There are more things in heaven and earth, Horatio,
Than are dreamt of in your philosophy.

Sweeping away skepticism is not the equivalent of kindling a saving faith. It may perhaps signify the forced opening of a closed mental door, but if nothing of substance is there to enter except on the superficial level of sensation, the whole thing is a waste of time.

Suppose Jesus had succumbed to this second temptation: "God has the power. Demonstrate it. Jump from that southeast tower of the Temple Cloisters straight down that four-hundred-and-fifty-foot drop into the Kedron Valley—in front of a hushed throng of thousands and they will see God's power as You descend unharmed!" Will they now? Is this how they will see that God loves them? Indeed no! The natural inference from such a spectacular display is, "Here is somebody who is specially protected by some power I do not have." The message is not, "A great God cares for me." Those watching such a feat would experience a sudden, upsetting, meaningless reversal of a natural law—the law of gravity. Their world would become less dependable.

Evil always wants God's power used for superficial sensation. Then it can be made to appear arbitrary and, as a result, meaningless. "Let God's power be spectacularly shown," suggests Satan. "No," says Jesus. "Your test does not begin to show it. Besides, you do not have the right to test God."

No one has. All those who make their belief in God dependent upon His jumping through the hoops of their deadlined demands have got it quite wrong.

*
**

God's presence and God's power are unmistakably revealed only to those who meet His requirements: that we
look, and look, and look again at the living, dying, and
rising of Jesus Christ. We must do it God's way or else we
are like primitive man trying to measure the ocean by
handfuls. We know not what we are measuring, and we
don't have the know-how to measure it. It is not that God
flunks our would-be tests of Him, but that He alone knows
what is being tested. So it must be done His way, in His
time, by His own test.

Jesus does not need the tempter to tell Him that God has
the power. He knows. For He has come to show it in no
shallow, spectacular fashion, but in God's way—a test
fraught with meaning and eternal truth.

Realize that the only time Jesus was high above the crowd
with all eyes upon Him was when He was dying a common
criminal's death. The chief priests and the elders jeered
Him, echoing the devil's temptation right to the end: "If
God is with you—jump! Leap down from the Cross and
we will believe you." Again He refuses. For this is God's
Love on the block, tested to the limit. And that involves
staying on the Cross: making the Divine identification with
the whole of humanity no wishful theory or fond hope, but
as real as the nails, the thorns, and the blood.

When the vast throng of mankind looks up to Him, they
do not see a specially protected, privileged superman whose
arbitrary use of a power they do not have somehow makes
their world less dependable. No. The Cross of Christ con-
firms for people the dark realities of the world then and
now—innocent suffering, cruel power, agonizing death,
rampant evil, and the unspectacular petering out of hope.
Whatever the blackness of any situation, look to the Cross
with wonder and realize He knows. God knows the worst
that has to be endured. In this lies the greatness of His
power—power not infinitely removed from us, but inti-

mately identified with us where it hurts, even to dying at our hand in our place.

Paul says:

> The preaching of the Cross is to them that perish, foolishness. But unto us who are called, it is the power of God and the wisdom of God.

Yes, His wisdom is the slow, "weak" power of Love. It is no manipulative moving and shaking worldly power. And that Love is forever demonstrated by the unspectacular, meaningful, total identification of God-in-Christ with the plight of us all. His way must be our way, if we would follow Him.

> Did we in our own strength confide,
>   Our striving would be losing;
> Were not the right man on our side,
>   The Man of God's own choosing.

> Dost ask who that may be?
>   Christ Jesus, it is He,
> Lord Sabaoth His Name,
>   From age to age the same,
> And He must win the battle!

O LIVING LORD, be with us as we focus on your Cross and see that you have done what only you could do for us, to free us from the power of sin and death; to find us in our lostness; to make us whole and bring us back to you in renewed life. Lord, bless us as we receive of your power and strength and love. Use us as a daily channel for these things in our world. Through Christ we ask it. AMEN.

8

The Image of Influence

At Rock Creek Cemetery for a burial, I noticed these words at one side of an elaborate tombstone:

> Power is greater than love.
> I did not get where I am by
> standing in line or being shy.

I suppose not! Such a person would probably not agree with the lines written by Arthur O'Shaughnessy over a hundred years ago:

> We are the music-makers,
>   And we are the dreamers of dreams,
> Wandering by lone sea-breakers,
>   And sitting by desolate streams:
> World-losers and world-forsakers,
>   On whom the pale moon gleams;
> Yet we are the movers and shakers
>   Of the world for ever, it seems.

People with the reins of power in their hands tend not to believe that, and consider themselves "the movers and shakers." They are usually too busy to listen to the solitary singer of a different tune; to catch sight of the distant dream glimpsed by the visionary; to hear the voice crying in the wilderness, "Prepare ye the way of the Lord."

Unfortunately, this is also true of many other people. They too will be unaware of, insensitive to, and unprepared for the great vision when it comes. For example: on a day one hundred and twenty-seven years ago readers of the morning's newspaper found only the briefest mention of a certain speech. The "news" judgment of that time evidently deemed it insignificant. Since then, the words have been graven not only in the hearts of the nation but in the marble of the Lincoln Memorial—the Gettysburg Address. Not many years ago, another man stood in front of that memorial, but the *Washington Post* in its lead story covering the event did not quote one word the man said. If he had a dream, they did not count it newsworthy.

Sad to say, much that is considered news is not about the farsighted movers and shakers, but rather the rearrangers of life—those who are engaged in a kind of perennial shell game in which they rapidly shuffle the three well-worn shells of "big bucks," "can do," and "know-how" in the hope that someday they will find under one of them the pea of mankind's moral progress. Fascinating maybe, but in my estimation ultimately futile. The intangibles, the things that don't compute, the nature of humanity, and the Spirit of God—the very essence of what the visionary sees and the dreamers dream—are left out of the reckoning.

*
* *

David S. Broder wrote of Martin Luther King, Jr.:

Almost everything he did in his life, from the Montgomery bus boycott to the final fatal march in Memphis was political. It was designed to challenge and change existing laws, customs and power. But the significance of his life was that the means he chose—passive resistance and passionate oratory—transformed and elevated the political struggle.

Yes, but why did he choose those means? Because his goal was not merely political or simply a confrontation with existing laws, customs, and power. Martin Luther King, Jr., whatever his failings, was a Christian pastor to whom, as to all Christians, was committed the Good News of God's reconciliation. This end determined the means he used. Power by itself can compel outward actions of compliance, but it cannot induce inward attitudes of caring. That takes an influence of a very different sort.

One congressman supporting the Martin Luther King, Jr. Holiday Bill recalled the civil rights struggles of the sixties in his own state of Arkansas. He went on to ask: "Do you know what we learned out of all that? The great changes are not made here in the legislative chamber or the judicial halls. The great changes of this world are made in the hearts and minds of men and women."

This truth is at odds with the perceived wisdom of those proudly practical people with their hands on the world's levers of power who reckon they know their stuff. They are like the doctor with a gruff sense of humor in one of G. K. Chesterton's "Father Brown" stories who says, "I'm afraid I'm a practical man and I don't bother much about religion and philosophy." Replies Father Brown, "You'll never be a practical man till you do!" And he is right. That which grips people's minds, motivates their acts, and changes their lives' direction is in the realm of the intangible—the sphere of the visionary, the songmaker, the voice from the wilderness.

Just before World War II, Macneill Dixon, professor of moral philosophy at Glasgow University, said in his book *The Human Situation:*

> It is by imagination that men have lived; imagination rules all our lives. The human mind is not, as philosophers would have you think, a debating hall. It is a picture gallery. Around it hang our similes, our concepts. . . . Metaphor is the essence of religion and poetry. . . . The prophets, the poets, the leaders of men are all of them masters of imagery; and by imagery they capture the human soul.

Yes. Take a moment to think of the images conjured up by the following phrases, and their effect on both world and individual histories: the Master Race; the Final Solution; the Empire on which the sun never sets; God's Own Country; a classless society; the American Dream; humanity come-of-age; the Evil Empire; a liberated "do-their-own-thing" person. These are largely twentieth-century concepts, most within the memories of us all. How potent these images were! But time evaluates their real worth and reveals insufficiencies, transience, half-truths, and outright lies.

Yet certain concepts and images have stood the test of time, not of a few decades or a few centuries but the test of the experience of millions over two millennia. For they accurately delineate the nature of humanity and its true context: the intangible and, ultimately, the only mover and shaker—God.

*
**

We have already looked at Jesus led by the Spirit into the wilderness to be tempted by the devil. We have studied the first two temptations in terms of the overriding question for Christ—and eventually for us—of how to do God's will. I believe that all three temptations can be seen as temptations to power. Christ's answers to the devil are not only guideposts for His Church pointing to the way it must take, but also perennially valid images of the truth about mankind, its Maker, and their relationship.

"You have the power, if you are God's Son" is implicit in the devil's first temptation. "Make the stones bread!" Had Christ yielded, if that were what it took to bring in the Kingdom, we would have no Gospel but rather a social gospel. Of course we know that equity, security, and freedom from want should be the practical concerns of Christians for others. But these concerns are an outcome of seeking God's Kingdom and His righteousness, not an alternative to them. Jesus was well aware of this, so His answer to the first temptation not only rejects the insufficient shortcut, but also gives us an image—a true image of our human nature: "Man cannot live on bread alone; he lives on every word God utters."

Here we have the image of a deeper hunger, something that cannot be satisfied by an abundance of material things. This hunger may be willfully denied, busily ignored, loftily dismissed, or cynically rationalized, yet it exists. God's will is that it shall be satisfied. The Christ who would not make stones bread says to a hungering humanity:

I am the Bread of Life. He that comes to Me shall never hunger. He that believes in Me shall never thirst; whoever comes to Me, I will in no way cast out.

In Him is met the hunger for forgiveness, the thirst for meaning, and the lostness of alienation. Mankind is more than body. This is the food of which we must eat to live eternally. This is the vital Bread the Church must share first in order to meet the deepest hunger of the world.

In the second temptation, the devil suggests: "God has the power. Leap! Leap down from the pinnacle of the Temple. He will save you. Demonstrate His power spectacularly." Again, Jesus refuses, "You are not to put the Lord your God to the test." Does this then place God in the category of a high government official refusing to take a lie detector test, thereby raising a large question mark in people's minds? No. Lie detector tests are far from conclusive evidence, and the same is true of all humanly devised tests of God. They are as arbitrary as the death-defying leap the tempter suggested, and just as meaningless.

God will reveal His power, yes. But God will reveal His power in His way. Jesus has come to show a famished humanity that God's nature is an all-embracing Love. He has come to demonstrate the power of this Love not by a spectacular leap down—even from the Cross—but by an unspectacular death. Jesus' rejection of the devil's shallow test is more than words. His whole life provides an image of a far greater test—God's test which reveals God's nature—the complete self-identification of the Divine Love with its object: a lost, hungering humanity. The Cross shows us the confrontation between God's Love and the subtlety of evil.

*
**

Says the tempter to Jesus in effect: "You have the power. Make the stones bread!" Refusing, Christ offers the image of a deeper hunger. Then the tempter says, "God has the power. He will save you. Jump!" Refusing, Jesus outlines by His whole life the image of the greatest test—the Cross.

Finally, the devil says: "I have the power. The power of all the kingdoms of the world is mine. It is yours if you worship me." Again, Jesus refuses with a Deuteronomic quote, "Thou shalt worship the Lord thy God, and Him only shalt thou serve."

I once read a reporter's account of a possible presidential candidate's view on a controversial issue. "He said that politically he's for it, but morally he's against it." The thought that playing down ethical demands and lowering standards leads to the road to power has occurred to others besides politicians. Is this the way the Church and individual Christians have to go in order to make an impact on the world? Must we trim or abandon tested conviction in pursuit of power?

If we acknowledge the example of Christ, this cannot be the way. Apart from anything else, how real, in the eternal scheme, will the gains of such power be? For the tempter's claim of having the power to give Christ the kingdoms is in itself a lie. It is the old overreaching claim of the world to be able to grant everything to its vassals. There is no mention of how limited, how transient, and ultimately how costly the offer really is. The deal involves the loss of one's own soul, one's true self, one's finest nature. It is an offer nobody can afford to accept. Christ warns there is no profit in gaining the whole world if you lose your own soul.

In the preface to his play, *A Man for All Seasons,* Robert Bolt says of Sir Thomas More:

He knew where he began and left off . . . but at length he was asked to retreat from that final area where he located his self. And there this supple, humorous, unassuming and sophisticated person set like metal . . . and could no more be budged than a cliff.

We live in a day where people, far from having a final area where they locate themselves, are struggling to find themselves. Lacking the gravitational pull of a solid core of tested conviction, they fly off in every direction. It is little wonder that they have a crisis of identity. They listen to the seductive hype of the world that promises it all, but actually delivers—at enormous cost—very little.

*
**

I began this look at the temptations by asking the question, How do we do God's will in the world? It is not by providing bread alone, but by awakening the deeper hunger which only Christ can satisfy. It is not by spectacular, meaningless sensation, but by declaring the power of God's Love for all humanity through that humbling death on the Cross. And it is not by losing one's soul in pursuit of power, but by the principled road of an enduring influence.

The simple fact is that the greatest continuing influence for good comes from the lives that have committed themselves wholeheartedly, freely, and gladly to the God revealed in Christ. Paul and St. Francis, Joan of Arc and John Wesley, Albert Schweitzer and Mother Teresa, Dietrich Bonhoeffer and Harry Emerson Fosdick—such people have no identity crisis, for they have no fear of commitment. Indeed, it is because in Christ they have seen and been influenced by His image of total devotion to God's will, that they know whose they are and whom they seek to serve. Who we are is inseparably linked to whose we are. We simply don't know who we are until we know to whom we belong.

"Thou shalt worship the Lord thy God and Him only shalt thou serve." The influence of those, known or unknown, who truly make that supreme commitment never stops. It goes far beyond them finding themselves. For they are found by God, then used by Him.

Cure Thy children's warring madness,
Bend our pride to Thy control;

Shame our wanton, selfish gladness,
    Rich in things and poor in soul.
Grant us wisdom, grant us courage,
    Lest we miss Thy Kingdom's goal.

How do we do God's will? We fix our eyes on Christ. We concentrate on the answer He revealed in a lifetime of showing the divine and lasting influence of God's love. We journey His road to His goal.

O GRACIOUS GOD, help us now as we strive to be true servants of your will in your world for our day. We are so often blind to you and your Presence because we are going our own road and doing our own will. Attune us to yourself. Make us channels of your mercy, reconciliation, and love, that as others see these qualities in us, it may have an effect, your effect, on the lives of people around. Through Christ we ask it. AMEN.

III

The Making of a Christian

9

From seeking to finding

The Constant Quest

Only a few decades ago, Joseph Stalin sneered, "And how many divisions has the Pope?" History is already revealing the folly of such prideful rhetoric. We have had the mind-boggling event of one of Stalin's successors, head of an avowedly atheistic state, visiting the Pope and promising that Christians in the Soviet Union would have the right to "satisfy their spiritual needs." Those very needs which at that moment did not officially exist.

Two hundred years ago, Voltaire, the rationalist, prophesied that the Christian faith would not last into the 1800s. Here we are, in the last decade of the twentieth century, and "The old, old story" is far from defunct. Indeed, Malcolm Muggeridge, the one-time man of the world who became a Christian, said as he reflected on the Christian faith's origin while making a film about Christ for the BBC:

There never was a story less over and done with. Following it, I was not delving into the past but peering into the future.

Why? Because theologies, policies, programs, forms, structures, or buildings are not the essence of the faith. These change. These decay. Yet certain creative factors at the heart of that story forever maintain their grip. Not because Christianity seeks to whet superstitious fear of the unknown, but because it best expresses people's deepest needs, highest yearnings, noblest acts, and non-self-regarding motives.

Paul once stood on Mars Hill and spoke to the wise ones of Athens. He said that God had created humankind of one blood, of one stock, for one purpose: "They were to seek God and, it might be, touch and find Him."

The constant quest is "to seek God and, it might be, touch and find Him"—Acts 17:27 in the New English Bible translation.

There is in humankind that which seeks its Creator, to touch and find Him. Christianity is *the* way whereby the seeker touches and finds. The Christian experience is that journey from groping in the darkness seeking ultimate reality to touching and finding it in God revealed through Jesus. Every gathering for worship is witness to the simple yet profound things that account for both our life as a Church and our daily existence as Christians. They are these.

*
**

First, a great need. No one ever begins to seek God out of a sense of complete self-content; only out of dissatisfaction and need. This is why those who hunger and thirst after righteousness are the happy ones, for only they find their deepest needs satisfied.

Some people think a need for God is a sign of weakness. They regard Him as a mental prop—a wish-fulfillment figure—whom His believers trust to take care of them. But wait! Is not the nature and quality of its needs the truest test of the status of any creature on the scale of existence? Certain forms of life require only the slime of the pool. People, however, need more than just food for their bodies, else they would be nothing more than animals. Mankind has a strange curiosity. He cannot live by bread alone. He must explore to the farthest star and build great telescopes to see what he cannot yet reach. That is the outward.

The inward is a divine discontent. The badge of human dignity, the sign of greatness, is an outreach for satisfaction without which humanity cannot rest content. We need music, books, art, and beauty, not just computers, jets, and telephones. We want ideals for ourselves and our society, a clear conscience, great purposes for which to live, and high faith by which to live if at our best we are to be content. Such expressions of need are inconceivable in an accidental bundle of atoms drifting to oblivion, which materialists tell us is the sum total of mankind. If we cannot accept such meaninglessness, then those needs for that which transcends the material are not a sign of weakness, but the mark of a deeper dimension to our being. And if, age after age, millions have sought God because they needed Him, then this is not a proof of immaturity but the admission of a basic yearning; a dim groping and a restlessness within.

Physically, we are so made that if our bodies have a specific deficiency, we will hunger for the very food that would make it up. In wartime Britain, bananas were almost unobtainable. For six years, when a rare shipment came in, they were restricted to one or two for children with green ration books—those under five years of age. How many older children and adults craved bananas in their need for potassium! This hunger is sure proof not only of our lack but also of the existence of food which will satisfy it. Likewise, when men and women seek more than the material, their search is proof not only of their need, but also of the existence of this spiritual food. Otherwise, why the craving?

People discover this great need in many different ways. It may be along the deceptive road of moral failure where they start off free to sin, only to discover that they are not free to stop. Remorse, guilt, self-despising, and eventual tragic consequences involving others is one road to a sense of need—the need for forgiveness, for the reestablishment of a right relationship. Many feel need through a sense of inadequacy in meeting the demands of life. Sickness, suffering, disappointment, and frustration are blows which make either bitter people or better people. It all depends on whether they have tried to cope without God or with Him. Sorrow and bereavement also lead to an admission of need. By whatever means we come to recognize it, mankind has, at heart, a great need.

Yet some would deny this, more's the pity. But then there are people who feel no need for music, books, or the sunset's beauty. This does not disprove the joy or the meaning in these things, but rather reveals the impoverished natures which cannot appreciate them. Similarly, what kind of person has no need for inward power to confront life's troubles, resist its temptations, and realize its opportunities? Does someone who acknowledges no such needs represent mankind at its best? I doubt it.

*
* *

If there is great need in mankind, it is fulfilled by a great salvation from God. In the constant quest there are millions of human hands stretched out in need, seeking fulfillment. Christianity tells of another hand outstretched in help.

Salvation is not a theory of how God acts to save us. It is the grasping of a proffered hand: being found when lost; being made whole when broken; a sense of God's inward peace in the place of dispeace; the upraising power of forgiveness when the weight of sin has gone. Salvation is knowing that God has acted in Christ for you and me; that we are no longer doomed to the darkness, alone, wandering and defeated. The Light is come!

Whatever words we use to express this, the experience means two things. One is a second chance. This is what God in Christ offers us. When we have failed or fallen, messing up life for ourselves and others with only the remnants of our first opportunities left, there is the amazing Good News of another chance. And who has not stood in need of the incredible miracle of forgiveness that reestablishes relationships as though they had never been broken, giving us a second chance?

Yet salvation is more than a second chance. It is also the strength to make something of it. Any kind of failure, especially moral failure, has a hypnotic, weakening effect which taunts: "You've failed. You're beaten. You cannot rise. You're done for!" It is then that we need One who not only lifts us up with a second chance, but empowers us to go on with a spiritual second wind until like Paul, in his Roman prison, we too can cry, "I can do all things through Christ who strengthens me."

Salvation is forgiveness, a second chance, power, the voice out of the darkness seeking the lost saying, "I am here. You can. You will. I shall help." This is precisely what Christ has meant to men and women over the years. Great need met by great salvation. No matter what the sophisticates may think, there is no gainsaying it.

*
**

The constant quest—the journey from seeking God to touching and finding Him—cannot be made without great gratitude. The early Christians called the Lord's Supper the

Eucharist, which simply means "Thank You." As in France they say, "Merci," and in Germany, "Danke," modern Greeks say, "Eucharisto." Hear it? Eucharist—thank you.

Why such gratitude? The Christian knows that if his hands have once stretched out and groped for the God who is not far from any of us, he has been found because another hand, outstretched and pierced, has already reached for him. God's Love moves first. If it did not, we would still be groping. Towers of Babel built up from below do not bring us closer to touching and finding Him. We could go to the stars and still be lost. For these are not admissions of our need, only boastings of our power. The whole Gospel is the story of the Divine searching and stooping down to a world of need—the sinners, the failures, the burdened, the lost. They know what it means to be saved.

The Church is unique because it is the only great company of people in the world who declare themselves sinners needing help (which is why we start our worship with a prayer of approach and confession); who welcome other sinners to the fellowship of the found. The Church is the gathering of the people of Christ who, knowing they are sinners, have faced their profound need, who have met with a profound salvation, and who go before the Cross of Christ to express a great gratitude to Him who first loved them.

G. K. Chesterton says in his poem "The House of Christmas":

To an open house in the evening
Home shall men come;
To an older place than Eden and a taller town than
    Rome.
To a place where God was homeless, and all men are
    at home.

From the beginning of time, God has wanted men and women to be at home with Him, that seeking they may touch and find. He prepares an open house for their help and need. This open house is His coming to us in Christ. It is the Incarnation. For there where God was homeless, all can be at home. But only because God in Christ was prepared to be homeless, despised, rejected, and acquainted with grief. That is the cost of our homecoming. Reflect on this today. For if we feel no great gratitude, we have not grasped what God has done, and we shall not go beyond vague spiritual gropings to sure touching and finding. We shall not discover the way home.

*
**

Great need, great salvation, and great gratitude are pointers along the path of the constant quest from seeking to finding. There is one more—great compulsion.

Compulsion is part of everyone's life. One way or another we are all coerced, for no one can escape the word "must." No one is free. Our only freedom is to choose our masters. But there is all the difference in the world between those who are mere creatures of circumstance, pushed and pulled by chance and fortune, subject to human command, and those whose compulsion springs from within.

Paul had one motive for all he ever did, one reason which made him endure shipwreck, flogging, and chains: "The love of Christ constrains me—compels me." Many since have known that same compulsion, not to be explained simply as doing good for the reward's sake, for convenience, or for conformity. Behind such compulsion is this thought: If, in your need, you have searched for One who has found you and lifted you up to newness of life at great cost to Himself, then you know you are His. The love that once sought you is the love that now drives you. Drives you to do His will—which is first and foremost loving God by caring for others.

These words were written by Albert Schweitzer from his hospital in Lambaréné, Gabon:

> The operation is finished and in the dimly lighted dormitory, I watch for the sick man's awakening. Scarcely has he recovered consciousness when he stares about and cries again and again, "I've no more pain." His hand feels for mine and will not let go. Then I begin to tell him that it is the Lord Jesus who has told the doctor and his wife to come here.

Friends, if only we obey the compulsion of Christ's love, then other searching hands grasping ours will know that they have touched and found His. Such is Christ's advent to His world.

Men and women were made for the constant quest—to seek God and, it might be, touch and find Him. They could do it through us if we have known great need, great salvation, great gratitude, and the compulsion of His great love.

There never was a story less over and done with than Christ's. For it must continue in you and me.

GRACIOUS GOD, who has laid your hand upon us that we might be useful to you in your world among your children; may we acknowledge our own great need, confess your great salvation, offer a glad, great gratitude for what you have done, and from now on be driven by the compulsion of your love in Christ. AMEN.

10

When faith falters

Doubtful Believer

We all know the cynical remark encouraging people to stick together in a venture, "If we don't hang together—we will hang separately!"

Real Christians of the most diverse type, character, and temperament can live and "hang" together in a truly amazing way. This was true of the first disciples: Matthew, the Roman hireling and taxgatherer; Simon, the Roman hater and Zealot; Peter, the impetuous; Andrew, the attentive introducer; Judas, the manipulator working secretly in the background. There was room for all kinds of temperament and interest. The one essential which brought and held them together was their love for Jesus.

The Church is a strange mixture because folk are a strange mixture. Christ calls all sorts of people. Only as they love Him are they able to love, understand, and make allowances for one another. Easter has just passed. There is a figure in that day's drama often used only as an illustration of one reaction to the Easter event—that of disbelief. Rarely is he focused upon for his character alone and what it reveals. I refer, of course, to the doubtful believer, Thomas.

Or, to give him his full title, the doubter who uttered the first creed.

Our text is John 20:26, the words, "And Thomas was with them." The man who doubted should be an encouragement to all those would-be Christians of the less confident, more pessimistic temperament.

There are two kinds of doubt. The first comes from a fundamental cynicism—the sour fruit of mean and careless living. Such a person is often strangely proud of his doubts. He wears them like medals as if his life were enriched by them. He doesn't keep an open mind or use his doubts as a doorway to some faith. He goes out of his way to find illustrations which strengthen them. In his heart he doesn't want to get rid of his doubts, for they are a ready defense against any awkward prompting to inward change of character or habit. So he puts on a sneer. He does not want to be convinced. He won't be convinced.

This is not the honest doubt of which Tennyson speaks in the lines:

> There lives more faith in honest doubt,
> Believe me, than in half the creeds.

It is not that Tennyson disparages creeds but that he recognizes that some people merely parrot a creed. They will simply repeat it without any conviction that the words are true, or that they believe them. But there are honest people who, if they cannot say something with assurance, will not say it at all.

This is the second kind of doubt—the honest person who will not say what he or she does not mean. Their integrity is such that they will not pretend to a faith they do not possess. The difference between the two categories is that the second would dearly like to have faith. They may be wistful and silent, wishing they could be sure. You can soon see their position because they will seek the truth honestly, "as blind men long for light." They will have looked their doubts squarely in the face, but they don't leave it at that. They search fully the other side—the case for faith.

Such a man was Thomas. Jesus always welcomes people like Thomas. "And Thomas was with them." What kind of person was he?

*
**

John's Gospel gives the most information about Thomas. In John 11 there is an incident that shows something of the measure of the man.

Jesus is beyond Jordan. He has left Judea where there is great hostility toward Him. John 7 gives the background to a situation which is still boiling. Then, the message comes from the sisters Martha and Mary that Lazarus, their brother, is very ill. They want Jesus to come to Bethany, just outside the city of Jerusalem where He knows danger awaits. Jesus delays for two days. Finally He says to the disciples, "Lazarus is dead. Now let us go." The disciples are horrified. "But your enemies will stone you if you venture back into Judea!" This is a critical moment in their time together. How will the disciples react to this suicidal course?

The first director general of the BBC, Lord Reith, used to say, "I do not like crises, but I like the opportunities they bring." It is the same with us. We don't like times of crisis. But they often bring rare opportunities. This was such an occasion. This crisis brought the opportunity for one man to stand out as spokesman. It wasn't Peter, the usual representative of the group—who talked before he thought. Here, Thomas speaks up with grim, courageous determination. "Let us also go, that we may die with Him."

In a way his is the highest kind of courage; not expectant

faith but loyal despair. No great expectation that something (like the U.S. Cavalry) will stage a rescue at the eleventh hour, but a loyal despair with no hope of betterment; facing the grim reality but not quitting.

Thomas was like that. He was an honest realist. He faced the ugly facts. He knew the chances. Christ's intention to return to Judea meant disaster. But Thomas would follow to the end. They all went back. Unfortunately, they did not stick it out to the bitter end. For as we know, at the bitter end in the garden of Gethsemane, "they all forsook him and fled." Yet Thomas had the root of the matter in him. His intentions were good. He may not have broken through the guard around the Cross shouting, "I am Christ's man. Let me die with Him." But he didn't mean to run away.

And that is like us. Often our intentions are good. But when the crunch comes, it proves too much for us. May Christ in His mercy pronounce over both Thomas and us what God said to David: "Whereas it was in thine heart— thou didst well that it was in thine heart."

*
**

The measure of Thomas? A good heart, a loyal resolve, a generous intent. Man considers the deed but God weighs the intention. We next hear of him in John 14. We see an apprehensive man, afraid of what the future will bring and afraid of misapprehending. The incident occurs in the middle of the well-known passage in which Jesus is speaking to His disciples in the upper room immediately before betrayal and crucifixion. Jesus knows what is in their minds. He speaks to reassure them:

> Let not your hearts be troubled. You believe in God, believe also in Me. In My Father's House are many mansions. If it were not so, I would have told you. I

go to prepare a place for you. And if I go and prepare a place for you, I will come again and receive you unto Myself; that where I am, you may be also. And whither I go, you know, and the way you know. . . .

Thomas butts in. "But we don't know where you are going! And how can we know the way?" Again, he speaks for the group.

The disciples are bewildered, so Jesus speaks to their anxious hearts. He gives them a poetic picture of His future care for them—a place prepared and a path prepared. They know the way. But Thomas, liking solid facts and fearful of not understanding poetry, blurts out, "We don't know the way!" He would never say that he has grasped what he has not. He is too honest and earnest to rest content with the vague and unsure. "The Father's house . . . many mansions. . . ." He does not know of any road to such a place. And so he expresses his doubts. Jesus might know where He is going, but Thomas does not. Death—oh yes, he can see that—the way they are heading. He has said as much before. But this comforting talk of reunion he cannot grasp. Jesus seems to assume they all know this road to the future. Thomas has to speak up—no doubt he speaks for the others as well.

The great thing is that by expressing his doubts, Thomas got a glorious answer: "The way?" answers Jesus. "Just follow Me. I am the Way—the Road to the Father."

Our apprehensiveness and fear of misapprehending can be of use if they come from an eagerness to grasp. If we are faithfully trying to understand and see the matter through, then God can answer our misapprehension and confirm that even the doubter asking, receives. It is worth remembering that the honest question of a doubting man evoked one of the greatest responses Jesus ever gave: Via, Veritas, Vita—"I am the Way, the Truth, and the Life." Thank God

the apprehensive Thomas with his fear of misunderstanding
was with the disciples then.

*
**

The third mention of Thomas comes in John 20. Here,
we have Thomas's big mistake. The incident took place on
the evening of the third day after the crucifixion. The room
was full of men fearful for their lives and disturbed by
strange rumors. The doors were securely fastened. Suddenly, Jesus was in their midst. Yes, Jesus Himself! Saying
to them, "Peace be unto you." A new courage, a new joy, a
new life flooded the room and charged like electricity
through the broken-hearted, defeated men.

What was Thomas's great mistake? He was not there.
Why? We can only guess. Thomas was courageous but, I
think, a natural pessimist. He had loved Jesus enough to
face death. He had expected the worst. Yet for all that, he
was possibly the more broken-hearted when it came. Like
many of similar temperament, he wanted to be left alone.

Britain's George V once said, "If I have to suffer, let me
be like a well-bred animal. Let me go and suffer alone." It
is true that we have to bear pain alone. But there are many
sorrows of mind and heart that are not best healed in
solitary confinement. We can keep to ourselves and shut
ourselves away, but that is a mistake. After a bereavement
people often do this. The wise course is to return to the
fellowship as soon as possible. For, by forsaking the house
of God, we may miss that word of Jesus, the very word of
comfort, blessing, and hope that would have best healed
our hurts. Thomas wasn't there when Jesus came. That was
his great mistake. For see what he missed. The Letter to the
Hebrews tells us that we should not forsake the assembling
of ourselves in regular worship. By failure to do so, many
have missed Christ speaking to them.

When Thomas heard the others' news, he felt it was too good to be true. When he heard the women's reports, he may well have thought that the morning was dark, and being overwrought, they were blinded by tears. When his fellow disciples told him excitedly of their experience, he put it down to hallucination born of frayed nerves and wishful thinking. It would take tangible evidence to convince him. Sounds crude and callous, but essentially Thomas was sincere and loyal to Jesus—even when he was convinced that there was no hope. But though he had no spurious hope to sustain him, he was as true to Christ as any of them; and he would remain so to Christ's memory.

Poor Thomas was away when the great thing happened. He didn't expect it to happen and he couldn't believe it when it did. And so the staunch skeptic spent seven more joyless, hopeless, restless days. How many have made the mistake of not expecting much to happen at worship? And when it did, they weren't there. They missed the word meant for them.

Charles Spurgeon was a great preacher of the nineteenth century. When he was a boy, he set off for worship one snowy Sunday. The road conditions became worse and he finally turned into a church that was handy but not his regular place of worship. The preacher had not been able to get through because of the snow. One of the members was pushed into leading the service. When it came to the sermon, the man announced as his text, "Look unto Me all ye ends of the Earth and be ye saved." The poor man repeated the text over and over because it was about as much as he had to say. "Yet," wrote Spurgeon, years later, "something happened to me at that service, during that sermon. For I looked and I saw and my life was changed forever."

Harry Emerson Fosdick, first minister of the Riverside

Church in New York, used to tell how in memory he would return to a little meetinghouse in a country town:

> It was a small, dilapidated structure when I was a boy
> . . . it preached a theology which I do not now believe,
> and insisted on denominational peculiarities in which
> I have not now the slightest interest. But one day in a
> pew of that church, I as a boy caught a glimpse of the
> vision glorious. . . .

We can never be sure that nothing will happen to us in worship. Our Savior promises that when two or more are gathered together in His name, He is there in the midst.

*
**

"And Thomas was with them"—if only he *had* been, the evening of that first Easter. We have seen something of the measure of the man—Thomas, the loyal and true, doubtful and afraid of not understanding poetry. We have learned— have we?—from his mistake of being absent.

What is the message of Thomas? John completes the story. A week later, Jesus came again. He offered Thomas the very test Thomas had specified. "Unless I see in His hands, the print of the nails, and put my finger into the print of the nails, and thrust my hand into His side, I will not believe." But when Jesus gave Thomas the opportunity, the sight of Him was sufficient to banish all doubt and melt his heart. Thomas fell to his knees crying, "My Lord and my God!" Jesus said to Him, "Thomas, because you have seen Me, you have believed. Blessed are they who have not seen and yet have believed." Thomas personifies the attitude of so many, "Seeing is believing." Christ's view is, "Believing is seeing. When you trust, you know."

Personal relationships cannot be analyzed in a laboratory.

They cannot be examined under a microscope. They must be experienced. To a large extent we have to enter personal relationships in trust. Only then do we discover their truth, not the other way about. So with Christ. As we trust, we know. As we believe, we see. His own rule states in John 7:17, "Anyone willing to do the will of God shall know the truth of the teaching." It is the same in the greatest relationship of all. We discover God in God's way, not ours. It is not a matter of "seeing is believing." For Christ's final beatitude is "Blessed are those who have not seen and yet have believed."

Although Thomas was a slow starter, in one bound he leaped over all the rest. He said to Jesus, "My Lord and my God!" The very first creed of the Church was three words: "Jesus is Lord." This was the creed of the Church by the time John's Gospel was written. There was no halfway house for Thomas. By that week after Easter his faith had arrived. "My Lord and my God!" He was not one who merely aired doubts. He doubted in order to become sure. And when he was sure, he went the whole road.

If we are depressed or pessimistic by nature, sometimes hopeless, often doubting, we can find encouragement in the doubter who uttered the first creed. For Christ will reveal Himself in His own way to you and me, until our faith is strengthened and we cry, "My Lord and my God!" Let us make sure that we are ready and waiting when Jesus comes.

John Wesley wrote:

> No one can truly say,
>   That Jesus is the Lord,
> Unless Thou take the veil away,
>   And breathe the living Word.
>
> Then, only then, we feel
>   Our interest in His blood,
> And cry, with joy unspeakable,
>   "Thou art my Lord, my God!"

"And Thomas was with them." The doubter believed!
"Do not forsake the assembling of yourselves together."
For the Lord Himself promises to be with us—here.

HEAVENLY FATHER, you know our need for faith. If we
have sought your gift and received it, however small it may
be, with you beside us it can yet move mountains. So grant
us grace to take that step forward that we *can* take in faith;
to find that we have strength for all the others. Through
Christ. AMEN.

11

Are you His friend?

Christian Consistency

It was in the British Army, into which I was drafted for three years as a callow youth of eighteen, that I met my first example of professing inconsistency. Said the sergeant-major, "Do as I say, not as I do!"

This lack of integrity, this lack of wholeness, is by no means confined to sergeant-majors. The word "integrity" comes from the Latin *in*, meaning "not," and *tangere*, the verb "to touch." Literally, not touched or defiled: untainted, entire, unimpaired, whole. Integrity is like death, virginity, or pregnancy—either you are in that state, or not.

Some people who make no profession of great spiritual truths may not bother much with consistency of word and deed. But when such profession is a person's *raison d'être*, as with some televangelists and moral leaders, then to lack integrity makes their lives a blatant denial and a poor example of the very power they profess and the truths they proclaim.

An educational article once asserted, "A profession of Christian faith is by no means a reliable guide to character." All I can say is, it should be! That it can be denied so confidently is an indictment of the thousands of so-called

97

Christians who have professed one thing and practiced another. This dichotomy, this division between what we say we believe and how we actually live day by day, is the most harmful disunity of all; far more harmful to the cause of Christ than denominational differences in Church government, for it is the basic disunity that makes the disbeliever scoff—the division in the individual Christian between creed and character, profession and practice.

Each one of us should ask ourselves how closely our being has matched our believing; how consistently our character has reflected our Christianity. If it has not, what can we do about it?

*
**

We would be greatly helped in this matter of Christian consistency if we realized afresh the essence of Christianity. It is not a matter of signing our names to a series of beliefs or valiantly trying to live out a set of commands. First and foremost, it is a relationship.

This is made abundantly clear in the question Jesus puts to Peter: A third time He said, "Simon, son of John, do you love Me?" Or, as appears in the footnote of the J. B. Phillips translation of those last four words in John 21:17: "Are you My friend?"

Are we His friends? For only a staunch friendship with Him will keep us from that terrible, inward, Christ-denying division in which our character does not reflect our profession of Christianity. If everyone who professed the name "Christian" were truly Christ's loyal friend, then no one would ever be able to say, "A profession of Christian faith is by no means a reliable guide to character." For it would be!

"Are you My friend?" Jesus asks us, one by one.

When we look back through life, we discover that most

of the things in ourselves of which we are either proud or ashamed have been put there by our friends: that particular friend of ours at home, at school, at work, or at leisure. The reality of such friendships is clearly seen in their influence upon us. The reality of Christ's friendship is bound to leave its mark upon us too. How does it happen?

The very fact that we know God wants our friendship and that He made us for fellowship with Himself tells us what being a religious person really means. It is not a mere front we adopt on suitable occasions, but a relationship with One we love. If our religion is a facade, then it will be no reliable guide to character; if it is a friendship, it is bound to affect our character as any deep friendship would.

If we want to live a life of Christian consistency, we must realize that there are laws governing friendships. Great human relationships do not just happen. There are conditions to be met.

*
**

The first law of friendship is the Law of Association. The friends who are most real to us and whose influence is greatest are those with whom we associate the most.

Think of that friend who once lived nearby. You saw him or her practically every day. You were close friends. You talked together, laughed together, and cried together. The influence of that life on yours was very real. Then the friend moved, perhaps far away. You wrote to each other but saw one another less and less. The months added up to years and while you would still count that particular person your friend, the day-to-day influence on your life was nowhere near as marked as it once was.

If two people are to form a deep friendship, they must take time to be together. This does not mean they have to see each other every day. Indeed, they may never have actually seen each other, as pen pals or ham radio operators the world over know. But there must be some regular form of contact.

We have never actually seen God in Christ, but the Law of Association still applies. If we wish to develop a friendship with Him, then we must spend time with Him in order to know Him better. Take your New Testament and let Him walk out of its pages as your daily companion. If you feel that the world and its affairs are much more real to you than God is, could it not be in direct proportion to the amount of time you are ready to spend reading the accounts of the world's doings and dilemmas in the newspaper? Would God not be more real to you if you spent a comparable amount of time reading the pages of His Book?

The other time-honored method of fulfilling the Law of Association with God is through prayer.

Someone once asked a wee boy if he said his prayers every night. "No sir," he replied. "Some nights I don't want anything!" This, unfortunately, is many people's idea of prayer: A "Hear, Lord, for Thy servant speaketh" rather than "Speak, Lord, for Thy servant heareth."

Yet if we have tested prayer in its truest sense, we have learned that it is not so much a way of getting things from God as of approaching God and receiving Him into our natures by opening up in two-way communication. Prayer is being at home with God; having an open door to the Almighty; showing hospitality to the Most High. "Are you My friend?" asks Jesus. We cannot be, if we hardly ever associate with Him.

*
* *

Friendship has another law—the Law of Expression. This simply means that friendship grows as we express our regard for one another.

We are made such that no thought, no feeling, no impulse is fully ours until we have expressed it. The more frequent the expression, the more complete the possession. The more often you express your love to your wife or husband, your children, or parents, the more real your love becomes. The more often you tell a friend of your admiration, the more that friendship will grow. And, of course, such expression will not only be found in your words, but in your actions. The cake you baked for a neighbor who was entertaining houseguests has strengthened a neighborly bond. The flowers sent to a sick friend; the visit paid to the hospital; the letter sent to bridge the gap between you and someone far away which took so much time to write; all these expressions of friendship have brought you and your friends nearer together.

Just as the parents who sacrifice for their invalid child find their love for that child growing ever deeper, so will you discover your interest strengthens as you show kindnesses to your friends. By the same token, as you express your friendship for God through acts of love for His children, so will your love for Him become "closer than breathing, nearer than hands and feet." Those who spend their lives wholeheartedly serving others for Christ's sake are the people most likely to be certain of the reality of God.

What do these laws of human friendship say to us? The first says that for friendship to form and develop, people must take time to be together in some way. The second tells us that our feelings for one another become more real and expand, the more we express them. Now if these laws apply on the horizontal plane of human friendships, you can be sure that they also apply on the vertical plane in relation to the God who made us in His own image for fellowship with Himself.

*
**

The third law of friendship is the Law of Commitment: committing ourselves to someone else in trust and dependence so that the more committed we are, the more we are in the position of supporting that person, or terribly letting them down. When it comes to human friendship, the latter possibility always lurks there—the betrayal of trust.

The classic example is Peter. He had fulfilled the Law of Association. For three years he had followed Jesus as His close companion. He also fulfilled the Law of Expression. He had declared his love and loyalty time and time again. "Though all betray Thee, yet will not I." But he does—in triplicate! No wonder Christ asks him three times, "Are you My friend?" Peter's final reply is, "Lord, You know everything. You know that I love You." And that is the truth.

Christ knows that even with the best intentions, we can let Him down. Yet He will never let us down—and this is what Peter discovers. Despite all that has happened, Jesus is still willing to entrust Himself and the all-important task of tending to His flock to someone like Peter. This is the wonder of the Divine Friend who "unlike our friends by nature, who change with changing years," is the One who never fails us and whose love never dies. Here is the Jesus who entrusts Himself to us, despite the wavering of our commitment to Him.

The legend tells of Christ's return to Heaven and how the angels surrounded Him, questioning Him about His terrible suffering for mankind:

"Does everyone now know how you loved them and died for them?"

"No. Only a few as yet, in a corner of Palestine."

"What have you done about letting the whole world know?"

"I've asked Peter, James, John, and the rest of them to tell others, who in turn will tell still others and spread the word of My love from person to person until everyone knows of it."

"But what if Peter and James and John forget? Or others fail? What if the years go by and men and women do not tell others about you and your sacrifice? What then? Have you no other plans?"

"No," said Jesus simply. "I'm counting on them!"

This is the miracle of His trust in us. He has no contingency plans. He depends on His friends. At that rate, it would seem a very chancy business. So it is, until His friends come to find, like Peter, that they can absolutely depend on Him to help them see it through.

"Are you My friend?" He asks each one of us now. We want to say "Yes." But knowing the great gulf that often seems to come between our ideals and our actions, and fearing that we may let Him down, we hesitate.

Hesitate no more. Jesus is asking you personally, "Are you My friend?" Answer "Yes!" and by association, expression, and commitment seek the friendship of Christ who will never let you down—the only Friend who can make our profession and our practice one.

> Dear Master, in whose life I see
> All that I would but fail to be,
> Let Thy clear light forever shine,
> To shame and guide this life of mine.
>
> Though what I dream and what I do
> In my weak days are always two,
> Help me, oppressed by things undone,
> O Thou, whose deeds and dreams were one!

ETERNAL GOD, you know how the prayers of our hearts may be different from the prayers of our lips. Grant that they may be one; that we may be made whole, and all our lives bear the sign, "Holiness unto the Lord." Through Christ we ask it. AMEN.

12

The Barnabas character

Son of . . .

However much religious faith may ebb and flow in any era, Christians, who have been around now for some two thousand years, will continue to be people worth studying. Why? Because they are refreshingly different. They do not merely follow the way of the world, adopt standard attitudes, or act from the usual motives. They are meant to be the salt that brings flavor to life and wholesomeness to society.

We are the Christians of today. We bear the name but do we have matching natures? If changes for the better are going to come in our world, they will not arrive miraculously from outside, but miraculously from within ourselves. Our natures will have to interpret the real meaning of our name.

The word "Christian" was first coined in Antioch, the third-greatest city of the ancient world. The locals there enjoyed a reputation for giving nicknames. When the bearded Emperor Julian visited them, they dubbed him "the goat." *Iani* was the suffix meaning "belonging to the party of." Thus the *Caesariani* were of Caesar's party. *Christiani* was a half-mocking, jesting, contemptuous nickname meaning "these Christ people." Yet the followers of Jesus accepted it gladly and made of it a name not of contempt, but of courage and love which all the world came to know. They did so through the quality of their living— still the only effective way to make a lasting impression. And their numbers grew.

How? Acts 11:24 tells us, "As a result, large numbers of people were added to the Lord." There is no decline in religion here. Perhaps if we study what brought this about, we could recreate the result.

*
**

Antioch was a beautiful, cosmopolitan city famous for both chariot racing and a deliberate pursuit of pleasure that went on night and day. In modern terms, it was a city of sport run mad, gambling, nightclubs, and loose living. With the Temple of Daphne located five miles from the city, "the morals of Daphne" was the ancient phrase to describe this lifestyle. Such a place as Antioch seems a strange setting for Christianity to take a giant stride forward, yet that is where the Gospel was first preached to the Gentiles without their asking.

It happened because after Stephen's murder and the subsequent persecution of Jesus' followers in Jerusalem, many fled to Phoenicia, Cyprus, Cyrene, and Antioch. In these places they preached with power to the Greeks and many became believers. When the headquarters in Jerusalem heard this, they sent the right man to help. Barnabas arrived. And "when he saw the wonderful things God was doing, he was filled with excitement and joy and encouraged the believers to stay close to the Lord, whatever the cost." Luke tells us that Barnabas was a good man, full of the Holy Spirit and strong in faith. "As a result, large numbers were added to the Lord."

Our modern world is very like Antioch. What we need is more of the Barnabas character among today's Christians. Then we might have some hope of the Barnabas effect, for if ever a man lived up to a good name, it was Barnabas.

The names Thomson, MacDonald, Smithson, and Macadam mean son of Thom, son of Donald, son of Smith, and son of Adam. Barnabas also means son of. . . . I leave the various translations to supply with richness and insight the nuances of his character. The New Testament in parallel columns gives us four versions: King James, Revised Standard, J. B. Phillips, and the New English Bible. Barnabas is first mentioned in Acts 4:36. The Revised Standard Version seems to sum up the Barnabas character exactly: "Barnabas, which means son of encouragement."

The word "encouragement" has at its root the thought of putting heart into a person. God knows there are enough things which take the heart out of people: illness, accident, frustrated hopes, sickening fear, empty loneliness, and sore grief. These are no respecters of locality or birth. In the world we see partisan, irreconcilable interests, the hopelessness of poverty and hunger, the apparent unwillingness of the rich to share, the daily obscenity of violence and drugs—all this on a planet where the environment is endangered, not to mention threatened by chemical and nuclear warfare. In the face of such things, an easy optimism is folly, tipsy hedonism empty, and human cleverness unavailing.

There is plenty to take the heart out of people. Surely what we need is someone to put it back in. Only one agent can adequately do this—the Spirit of God, promised by Christ. The Holy Spirit produces the Barnabas character in the individual and the Barnabas effect in the Church to which, as a result, large numbers are added. If we want the Barnabas character, we must have the Barnabas spirit. We cannot put heart into others from our own divided hearts.

In the musical *West Side Story* there is a love song of deep dedication:

> Make of our hands, one hand.
> Make of our hearts, one heart.
> Make of our lives one life.
> Day after day, one life.
> Now it begins. Now we start—
> One hand, one heart.

When we can reverently say the same to God—one hand, one heart with His—we then have the Barnabas character. We are sons and daughters of encouragement.

*
**

What does this mean in everyday terms? It means a life where hand and heart are integrated. The late George MacLeod, founder of the Iona Community, used to say:

> The quickest way to symbolize integration is by the gesture of two hands interlocked. The right hand of worship and the left hand of work . . . the right hand of Sunday and the left hand of weekday.

When the right hand of our belief and the left hand of our acts both interlock, you have an integrated life.

Let the Lord be at your right hand. Make it one with your left in daily deed, and the most powerful influence in human life is present. Without uttering a word, such living exhorts others to climb new heights of God-discovery.

This was Barnabas—a whole person. He did not profess one thing and do another. He was no poor alienated soul separated by sin from the things that belonged to his peace. He was one hand, one heart with God, and the result showed in practical ways. When there was real need in the young Church, the affluent gave generously to help others. This was not charity compelled by law but by love. Barnabas sold a plot of ground he owned and donated the entire proceeds. The money, however, was not a substitute for the giving of himself. He had given himself already; his heart belonged to Christ. Now, as all could see, so did his hand.

In the third century, Clovis and his Franks embraced Christianity. In those early days, whole armies were baptized at once in a river. An unfortunate practice, for many warriors entered the water holding their right hands high above their heads, keeping them clear of the water—each could then say, "This hand was never baptized" and reckon himself as free as ever to swing a battleaxe. Shocking hypocrisy for so-called Christians! Yet we, too, know Christians who have been baptized—all but their bankbooks, their weekend sports, their business methods, their pleasures, or their tongues. Might they even be ourselves?

Barnabas was a son of encouragement because his heart was whole, one with his hand. His entire life preached without words, exhorting all who knew him to a deeper dedication. Thus the New English Bible identifies him as "Barnabas, son of exhortation." This is one strand of encouragement. Other people were encouraged by the witness of his whole heart exhorting them.

***

As well as a whole heart, Barnabas had a brave heart. Look at the situation described in Acts 9 in which Paul (the former persecutor Saul) found himself. He had come to Jerusalem but the disciples were all afraid of him. They did not trust his conversion. Had it not been for the brave heart of Barnabas willing to take the risk and believe that Paul's was a genuine conversion, what would have happened? Paul might well have gone away hurt and disillusioned. One dreads to think how many people, for far less reason, have left the Christian fellowship, unwelcomed, hurt, and disillusioned, simply because there was no Barnabas around.

Men and women often need the kind of consolation that Barnabas gave to Paul. Condemnation is no help. They need someone who will believe in them day after day; someone who will accept them, trust them, and take a risk for them—the risk of being laughed at, conned, thought naive; the chance of being let down, unpopular, or snubbed. Only the brave heart takes the chance and only the brave heart brings consolation.

The King James Version reads, "Barnabas, son of consolation," another strand of encouragement. When he met Barnabas, consolation was the encouragement Paul needed. Could we offer similar encouragement to others, if we were brave enough to take the risk? Barnabas of the whole heart was a living exhortation. Barnabas of the brave heart was a ready consolation.

*
**

Finally, Barnabas had a glad heart. When he went up to Antioch and saw the wonderful things God was doing there, he did not go about with a frozen expression, taking notes, jotting down statistics, and looking wise. We read, "He was filled with excitement and joy and encouraged the believers to stay close to the Lord, whatever the cost." No wonder that, as a result, "large numbers were added to the Lord."

Obviously there was an enheartening, comforting—in the sense of strengthening—spirit about Barnabas. The Latin root of the word "comfort," *fortis*, means brave or strong. And this is how J. B. Phillips describes him: "Barnabas, son of comfort"—the comfort that makes strong.

When his glad heart saw the good work, he expressed his joy freely and his very attitude was a tonic to their spirits. "This is wonderful," he said. "I am so happy for you. Stand by the Lord and He will never let you down." And the work went forward by leaps and bounds with his glad encouragement.

How the Church of today needs the Barnabas character! It is crying out for the whole heart that exhorts, the brave heart that consoles, the glad heart that comforts and strengthens. If every minister, if every member, were a Barnabas, there would be no holding back Christ's Kingdom. But that can never happen until each of us is "one hand, one heart" with the Spirit of God.

Are you a son or a daughter of encouragement?

> Love divine, all loves excelling,
> Joy of heaven, to earth come down,
> Fix in us Thy humble dwelling,
> All Thy faithful mercies crown!
> Jesus, Thou art all compassion,
> Pure, unbounded Love Thou art;
> Visit us with Thy salvation,
> Enter every trembling heart.

ALMIGHTY GOD, we bless you for your love shed abroad in the world and in the lives of people whom we have known. They, by their influence, have touched our lives and made us different through the knowledge we came to have of you. Bless us now. Lay your hand upon us that we may be an extension of your voice, your hand, your heart. So may we do the work of a Barnabas here in your world. Through Christ we ask this. AMEN.

IV

For Daily Living

13

The French have a word for it . . .

A Matter of Style

Some time ago two different styles of living were featured in the press. The first concerned the then ongoing saga of Donald Trump and his wife who had signed an agreement that for sixty days they could behave as if they were single and nothing either did during that period could be used as grounds for divorce. This might be called "a moratorium on morals" or "no-fault hanky-panky." The other reflected our First Lady's lifestyle as influential wife, mother, and grandmother. One hundred and fifty seniors at Wellesley College signed a petition objecting to Barbara Bush as their commencement speaker. To these presumably brightest and best such a role model was apparently limited in goal, curtailing and compromising their ambitions. They had an arrogant intolerance toward marriage and motherhood being held up as a worthy endeavor. It did not fit in with their own narrow preconceived agenda.

These instances reveal a great lack of awareness. The good life is not "me-centered" but "other-centered." Morality and family are the cement of society without which it disintegrates. People who dismiss these ideas as out of fashion only show how far their "me-centered" style of life detaches them from the realities of life. Catastrophe awaits them down the road.

As Christians we must have a very definite style of living and realize with what manner, bearing, and attitude we should face life. The word that best sums up how we Christians should live is one which is now out of fashion and consequently misunderstood. It is the word "meek."

"Blessed are the meek," says Jesus, "for they shall inherit the earth."

"Yes," says the cynic, "and that's the only way they'll ever get it. And once they've gained their inheritance, let's see how long they can keep it."

Speaking of Jesus in the preface to one of his plays, George Bernard Shaw writes, "Even St. Luke, who makes Jesus polite and gracious, does not make Him meek." Shaw cannot have read his New Testament too carefully, for the Christ who calls the meek "blessed" says of Himself, "I am meek and lowly in heart. . . ."

Obviously the word has lost its original meaning. Pious submissiveness and weak-kneed tameness do not inherit the earth. It was not a deficiency in spirit or courage which brought Christ to the Cross. Yet meek, I maintain, is the Christian style of living. So what does it mean?

*
**

As a guide, let us look to the original Greek word *praotes*. Aristotle defined a virtue as the happy medium between two extremes. For instance, if miserliness is one extreme and utter squandering the other, then generosity is the virtue between. Consequently, *praotes* (translated as meekness) is the virtue that lies halfway between excessive anger and extreme angerlessness. Indeed it has some element of being angry—at the right time. When is the right time to be angry? As a general rule, when the anger is directed at injustice or injury done to someone else. Selfless anger over the sufferings of others is a great dynamic force for good. "Me-first" anger, concerned only with ourselves, is sin.

But that is only one facet of the meaning. The Greek word *praotes* is also used to describe an animal trained to obey commands and taught to accept control. Combining these two thoughts we have a new concept—forcefulness under control; power held in check and rightly directed. Such a definition makes sense of the Bible's use of this outmoded word "meek." The controlled power of Jesus and the rightly directed, nicely judged forcefulness of His followers are most desirable as a lifestyle. Such meekness should be the mark of the Christian. Yet this is not the whole story.

I keep stressing the word "style," for it is evident both from the Gospels and from history that Christ's followers had, as we say, "a way with them." Indeed they were followers of the way of Jesus Christ who is the Way. It showed in their everyday walk. Their lives had a certain style that people couldn't help noticing. Even the professional men on the Jewish Sanhedrin were astonished by the attitude of the prisoners brought before them. Uneducated laymen they might have been, but they had something, a *je ne sais quoi*, a fearless poise, a steadfast gaiety. The Council members realized that these men were former companions of Jesus. This then was the explanation. They were infected by His way.

The French have a word for it which pictures the attitude exactly—*débonnaire*. That is how the Greek *praotes* (meek) is translated in a French New Testament. How different it sounds! "Happy are the debonair—they shall inherit the earth."

Perhaps you feel this suggests the elegance and *joie de vivre* of Maurice Chevalier. This may seem a strange picture of the Christian, but in essence it is far nearer the truth than any word linking the faith of Christ to mere submissiveness, timidity, or apprehension.

The debonair have style. Obviously there is a style that is purely superficial, no deeper than manners and dress. Fashion is style on the outside. Faith is style on the inside which shows on the outside. The meek, the debonair, are those whose inner lives are clothed with the stylish fabric of Christian faith which never goes out of fashion, designed for life by Jesus Himself.

Listen to the prophet's words applied to Christ as He enters Jerusalem that first Palm Sunday: "Behold thy King cometh unto thee, meek. . . ." Debonair—literally, "of good aura, spirit, or bearing." How attractive is this nonmilitary monarch! He needs none of the pomp and panoply the world's rulers often require to bolster up the petty mind, the brief authority to conceal the midget soul. For this is Greatheart. He has not come to assert the Jews' pride of race, or ape the Romans' pride of power, or vie with the Greeks' pride of intellect. Others may be harsh, self-assertive, covetous, or dictatorial but such is not His style.

The meek, like their Master, have a certainty born of trust in God and His wise overall purpose and eternal truth. Thus assured, they are Christlike and debonair in the face of discourtesy, injustice, lies, and hatred. They remain under God's supreme control, unruffled and meek, with fearless poise and steadfast gaiety. They have a lifestyle second to none.

*
**

Paris fashions for a new season are kept a closely guarded secret until their unveiling. The Christian lifestyle is an open secret. The fabric of the faith has been on display for some two thousand years. Wearing it, the most ordinary souls are transformed. The fabric of the faith never dates.

Why? Because joy from within is never out of fashion, and the spiritually debonair "have a way with them" in any century.

Listen to Isaiah, turned fashion writer, extolling God's New Look for mankind:

> Let me rejoice in the Lord with all my heart, let me exult in my God; for He has robed me in salvation as a garment and clothed me in integrity as a cloak.

This wondrous garment is of God's righteousness not our own. We cannot buy it. As the hymn writer says:

> Mine is the sin, but Thine the righteousness;
> Mine is the guilt, but Thine the cleansing Blood;
> Here is my robe, my refuge and my peace;
> Thy Blood, Thy righteousness, O Lord my God.

If we continue the metaphor of clothing and style, then this robe of God's goodness shows some dramatic effects in the lives of those trusting Him—startling apparel of transparent effect. No, not like Hans Christian Andersen's story of the Emperor's New Clothes which didn't exist. The transparent quality is absolutely real and shows in the "see-through" character. The robe of God's righteousness produces the pure in heart, who alone can "see through" to God as they themselves are transparent in goodness. These are the people whose basic inner truth and authenticity shine through in everything they do and say. While others recognize this translucence, those who have it are so intent on seeing more of God, they are unaware of the effect on themselves: nobler living, purer motives, simpler faith, and greater goals. These traits shine through, for such is the effect of being clothed with the garment of God's Grace. Purity of heart gives transparency of character.

Moreover, the cut of this robe is generous. Jesus says:

There must be no limit to your goodness. You must be
all goodness, just as your Heavenly Father is all good
. . . if you greet only your brothers, what is there
extraordinary about that?

The Christian is called upon to display the extravagant
goodness of God. And this is no skimpy robe, but one
which covers all. His love covers a multitude of sins,
according to Peter, when we let it clothe our lives. For His
love always goes beyond the worldly calculations of what is
sensible, fair, expedient, and wise. He would never have
loved us in the first place on any of these grounds. God's
goodness to us in Jesus is, as we say in Scotland, "daft"—
inexplicable by any human measurement. And it is with a
comparably extravagant style of loving that His true followers live.

Think of Albert Schweitzer, in his thirties already on his
way to greatness in three fields—theology, music, and philosophy. What does he do? Turns his back on the glittering
prizes of Europe to become a missionary doctor in equato-
rial Africa. "Daft! Extravagant waste!" say those who have
calculated all the percentages. What does their verdict matter, if the Master's word is "Well done, good and faithful
servant." That's the style!

*
**

Look at this beautifully cut garment of God's righteousness as it stylishly wraps around the debonair with the
transparency of character and the generous cut of an extravagant goodness, and colors life with selfless caring. "By this
shall all know that you are my disciples," says Jesus, "if ye
love one another."

Unfortunately, that overworked word, "love," can mean anything from the excesses of Hollywood to the Kingdom of Heaven. As Archie Craig, a former moderator of the Church of Scotland, once wrote:

> The word love always needs a dictionary and for Christians the dictionary is Jesus Christ. He took this chameleon of a word and gave it a fast color so that, ever since, it has been lustered by His Life and teaching, and dyed in the crimson of Calvary, and shot through with the sunlight of Easter morning.

Here is the color of the Love of God. The robe of His righteousness shimmers with the hue of holiness, the shade of sacrifice, the tint of eternity. Its color is fast, unfading, and permanent.

Blessed are the debonair—transparent in character, extravagant in goodness, their whole lives shot through with caring. These are not the "me-centered." Put on the robe of God's righteousness and become one of them. For eternal living, that's the style!

———————————

HEAVENLY FATHER, your love is upon all, the good and bad alike. You want the best for each one of us and your love is no soft, easy sentimentality but the strong, unconquerable goodwill of one who is not willing that any should perish but that all should find their life in you. Help us to wrap the robe of your righteousness around our lives in transparency of character and care for others. May we concentrate on living your love every day. For Jesus' sake. AMEN.

14

More than feel good

When Worship Works

A missionary from Africa told me the story of a rather stern teacher in a school there who was training a class of boys for a music festival. The choral test-piece was a gypsy song in which the words "Ha! Ha! Ha!" kept recurring. The teacher asked a lady who was something of an expert on choral singing to listen to their performance and give her verdict. "Very good," she said. "Their only problem was—they didn't smile when they sang 'Ha! Ha! Ha!'" "Right," responded the teacher somewhat grimly. "I'll make sure they smile."

Many feel that worship falls into this category—a big act in which some none-too-jolly people are cajoled or exhorted to appear cheerful. Worship definitely calls for joy, but it must be the real thing. Our joy must spring from the depths of experience. It must be neither an untried superficial gladness nor a big act of enforced cheer—pretending to feel what one does not. Worship will not work in that fashion. On the other hand, neither will it work if it is made into a matter of mere feeling.

I once attended a service where, after the Call to Worship,

an excellent jazz pianist accompanied a blues singer in a
solo rendition of "To be free," as the opening praise:

I wish I knew how it would feel to be free.
I wish I could break all those chains holdin' me.
I wish I could say all those things I should say,
   Say 'em loud, say 'em clear
   For the whole round world to hear.

I wish I could live like I'm longin' to live.
I wish I could give all I'm longin' to give.
I wish I could do all those things I'd like to do.
   Though I'm way overdue,
   I'd be startin' anew.

I wish I could fly like a bird up in the sky.
How sweet it would be, if I found I could fly.
You know, I'd soar up to the sun and look down at
   the sea.
   Then I'd sing 'cause I'd know
   How it feels to be free.

It had a good beat. As pious entertainment, it was fine. As
a "me-centered" musical monologue, it was okay. "I wish
. . . I wish . . . I wish. . . ." But as worship, it was a failure.
The whole piece was entirely subjective, a yearning for
spiritual "feel-good." Neither God nor Christ got a mention. But then They are not needed if we assume that
worship is the religious equivalent of "wishing upon a star."

*
**

Is this worship? Our feelings? Our moods? Our prefer-
ences? Our tastes? Contemporary phrases and praises designed to catch our attention? I know that the subjective

side is a necessary part of worship. Styles of worship and liturgies may be useful vehicles in transporting grace for our needs, but they never get out of the groove simply by our changing the phraseology and fashioning new forms. They must be powered by a real awareness of God's Presence. With His Spirit energizing them, even the most familiar, time-worn words will come alive.

The distinguishing feature of true worship is an objective focus on Christ. Thus worshipers, with courage and initiative, are enabled to deal with reality.

It is a tribute to the religious genius of the Hebrews that the same word denoted work, service, and worship—the word *abad*. In biblical thought there is no watertight compartment between daily work and the adoration of God. Work and worship are the same word—with God's Spirit energizing both. Indeed, the aim of worship is not to remind men and women of how they may feel about their woefully inadequate good works. The aim is to remind people of the mighty works of God on which our very existence, our redemption, and our final fulfillment depend.

True worship links today with yesterday and tomorrow. It lets believers know whence they came, and whither history is leading them. It sets before them at the same time both the wonderful kindness and the holy demands of God. Good works must never be a substitute for worship, but its outcome. Good works are the complement of true worship—its natural reflex.

What makes worship work? To answer, I want to look at the text of John 16:33. Jesus is speaking to His disciples:

In the world you will have trouble. But courage, the victory is Mine; I have conquered the world.

*
**

Worship works when it faces reality.

The capacity to worship is something God has given to human beings alone. This ineradicable desire to enthrone someone or something is a mark of our humanity. Unfortunately, mankind has often erred by worshiping the false and foolish, the dissatisfying, and the deceitful. Because our natures are molded by what we admire, we humans have often been less than our best by venerating the inferior, the transient, and the insufficient. The true test of whatever we worship is its adequacy in the day of trouble. It is then we discover that our idols have feet of clay.

"Don't worry, it may never happen" is no Christian message. "In the world you will have trouble," says Jesus to His handful of bewildered followers shortly before His betrayal. Here is no starry-eyed sentimentalist who thinks that evil will flee at the first blows of a few good intentions, or that heart-chilling fear will be vanquished by the power of positive thinking.

"You will have trouble," Christ warns *us* also. Nothing is going to be easy. There will be no exemptions because we are His followers; no simple solutions. The world is that kind of place—full of troubled, alarmed, and desperate people with disquieting, even disastrous, possibilities always crowding in upon them. Age sets in or illness threatens; unforeseen change devalues or deprives; those dear to us hurt, fail, or make a shipwreck of their lives—the list is endless. Fear clutches with cold hands a world in which many seem to have lost their nerve for living, as science outstrips morality and what we know far exceeds what we understand; as our power to accomplish gross evil grows far beyond our will for goodness.

Worship must face such reality because Christ faces such reality. In the world—trouble. It is from a troubled world that we come to worship One who faces its reality; who not only faces it, but is sufficient for it. Surely one element of worship must be our need—driving us to Him who stands when every false idol falls.

*
**

"In the world you will have trouble. . . ." When worship works, it faces reality; the very reality that brings us here to worship Christ who alone is able to confront sin, fear, and death. But moreover, when worship works, it produces joy. "In the world you will have trouble"—yes. "But be of good cheer," the King James Version says. "Courage!" the New English Bible translates.

Obviously, the New Testament idea of joy is not merely a matter of shallow gaiety which can be shattered by devastating events. Christian joy is independent of circumstance and is grounded in the quiet courage that comes from our relationship with the indomitable Christ. Joy is the flashing facet of an indestructible jewel whose other surfaces are peace, patience, kindness, goodness, faithfulness, gentleness, self-control, and love. This jewel is the Spirit of Christ. We cannot select the joy alone. For all these virtues, as Paul says, are the fruit—not fruits—of the Spirit. We cannot have the joy, without Him; having Him, we cannot be without the joy—even in a world of trouble.

A man who set his name to the Antislavery Declaration of 1833 was hated as a radical, misrepresented in the press as a traitor, and pelted with rotten eggs when he went to speak at an antislavery meeting in Concord, New Hampshire. Yet such was his inner strength that John Greenleaf Whittier could write such verses as:

> Here in the maddening maze of things,
>   When tossed by storm and flood,
> To one fixed ground my spirit clings,
>   I know that God is good.

In joy of inward peace, or sense of sorrow over sin,
He is His own best evidence; His witness is within.

And again,

> Drop Thy still dews of quietness,
>   Till all our strivings cease;
> Take from our souls the strain and stress,
>   And let our ordered lives confess
>   The beauty of Thy peace.

This is the essential joy no one can take from us, for it is built on the courage Christ bids us claim as our trust is in Him. This is what worship should produce in us—a grasp of God, a confidence in Christ. This is the how of worship—not just on Sunday but every day—so that we carry with us the divine infection of a good courage, showing a steadfast joy in the face of every reality, as we obey the One who bids us "Be of good cheer!"

*
**

"In the world you will have trouble." When worship works—it faces reality. "But courage." When worship works—it produces joy. "The victory is Mine; I have conquered the world." When worship works—it enthrones the Victor.

This is the chief object of worship—worth-ship! This is what it is all about. We extol God's worth. We hail the power of Jesus' name. We confess with our lips and our lives that He is worthy of our adoration and praise. He is worthy of our turning to Him for courage—for He will give it; worthy of our gratitude—for He has done it; worthy of our approach in prayer for others—for now we ourselves are showing something of the love with which He first loved us.

Worthy is the Lamb that was slain and hath redeemed us to God by His blood; worthy to receive power and riches and wisdom and strength and honor and glory and blessing.

If we do not enthrone Christ as Victor in our worship by whatever words we use, then—God help us—we will never live victoriously out in the world. He is Victor. He is no Napoleon making off in that ghastly retreat from Moscow, securing his own safety while leaving his troops to perish miserably in the bitter cold. Christ has never deserted us—though we have deserted Him. Whatever He promises, He fulfills. In the face of that lonely Cross, where the Love of God confronts the sin of mankind, He says: "Courage. The victory is Mine." And it is.

> Rejoice, the Lord is King:
>   Your Lord and King adore!
> Mortals, give thanks, and sing,
>   And triumph evermore:
> Lift up your heart, lift up your voice!
> Rejoice, again I say, rejoice!

"In the world you will have trouble. But courage, the victory is Mine; I have conquered the world." Reality. Joy. Triumph! These are present when worship works.

———————————

HOLY LORD, lift up our hearts within us that they may chime with our voices as we hail your victory, acknowledging you to be the Lord who has done for us that which we could not do for ourselves; who has faced the reality of human sin and death and defeated it, thereby giving us cause for joy and courage. In the knowledge that you are the final Victor, help us to live victoriously in the here and now as our tribute to your triumph. Through Jesus Christ our Lord. AMEN.

15

Dealing with anxious fear

Fear and Faith

What scares you? Of what are you afraid? Nearly everyone, even those with strong, aggressive personalities, harbors some fear, secret or confessed. It may be of darkness or depth, of crowds in a broad place or restriction in a narrow space.

From the Greek word *phobos,* psychologists have coined a whole jargon to label our fears. There are more than seventy-five phobias listed in the dictionary, ranging from agoraphobia (fear of public places) to erythrophobia (fear of blushing) to phobophobia (the fear of fear itself). And that is not imaginary. As Franklin D. Roosevelt said in the early 1930s, "The only thing we have to fear is fear itself."

There is no doubt that we live in a fearful world. As fear of sudden nuclear cataclysm diminishes, fear of slower ecological disaster will no doubt replace it. There is fear of unemployment as businesses collapse, economies change, and machines increasingly replace the need for human skills. Fear of failure can haunt men and women from their first tests at school. As life goes on, many people fear a breakdown in health through accident or disease. Some, as they grow older, fear death. Yet these fears are not neurotic imaginary anxieties without cause. They are real enough.

In a way, fear has a positive side. If a child does not develop a few healthy fears like the fear of traffic dangers, ill-intentioned strangers, boiling kettles, deep water, and bottles labeled "poison," he or she may not get the chance to develop at all. Fear which points to safety is one thing, but fear which oppresses the soul, quite another. Fear is an integral part of the human situation with specific causes which must be faced, analyzed, attacked, destroyed, or, if need be, endured.

*
**

Either we deal with our fears or they deal with us. I want to look at these alternatives as they are outlined in Psalm 27. That psalm is the personal testimony of one who has run the mental gamut of fears, faced them, and found the answer. Throughout the psalm we see a variety of fears, and though, as scholars point out, this could be a composite poem by more than one person, the psalm has the unifying theme of God's relationship to human fear.

Whether we interpret them metaphorically or as actualities the writer had to face, the fears are all there. He speaks of the wicked closing in to devour him; the time of trouble; the forsakenness of being left alone in the world; the watchful foes and malicious liars awaiting their chance to overthrow him. There is nothing outdated about the psalms' portrayals of human nature and need. Whoever the author, he knew the meaning and all the symptoms of fear: the dry mouth, trembling hands, weak knees, and quaking heart.

But this is only one side of the psalm. Interwoven throughout is a confession of faith. Indeed, it is in the light of this faith, that these fears are put in perspective. He begins:

> The Lord is my light and my salvation;
> Whom shall I fear?
> The Lord is the strength of my life;
> Of whom shall I be afraid?

Then he goes on to list his fears. Yet each is followed by an assurance: God will bring him through, keep him safe, set him on a rock, not forsake him, give him guidance. Note that he does not declare that God will remove the causes of his fears, but that He will give him the inward resources to deal with them.

This psalm is about the God who enheartens us: the One who puts courage into an individual, stiffens the backbone, gives a "second wind" of spiritual stamina, and strengthens the heart.

In this century of secularization, when men and women debate what it means to be religious, some theologians no longer believe in a living God who is an Entity apart from His Creation and who works personally in human life and history. They tell us that God is not a person who loves but that God is love—the sum total of all the love in human life—and that we deal with this God through loving involvement in the lives of others and not through the formal practice of religion. Thus, in their view, it is not a matter of drawing apart in prayer or worship that brings real contact with God. Such thinking would suggest that Jesus could have spent His time better not going up a mountain to pray, and that the Psalmist was mistaken in his desire to have a lifelong fellowship with God, "seeking His face and inquiring in His temple."

God may be far more than personal, but He is certainly not less. I feel strongly that the Psalmist's conscious effort

to live close to the living God did for him what much
modern theorizing singularly fails to do—it worked! It put
new heart into him. It helped him deal with his fears,
ennobling his life.

In Psalm 27:13 he says plainly, "Unless I had believed to
see the goodness of the Lord in the land of the living!"

As it stands, the sentence is an exclamation. Something
has to be supplied at the beginning of the verse to bring
out the meaning. The King James Version inserts the words,
"I had fainted. . . ." This is the implied alternative to the
Psalmist's trust in the goodness of God. Unless he had
believed, he would have fainted. Reflecting on the inspired
phrase the translators supplied, we can see the good sense
in it.

*
**

Physical fainting can be brought about by sudden fear.
When the worst has happened and it is more than someone
can take, they pass out. Spiritual fainting is much more
deadly—an inward faint-heartedness when stamina goes,
courage drains away, and there is a capitulation into moral
unconsciousness. For every one person who faints physically, there are scores who faint spiritually. And how many
of these are so-called Christians? The inner fires of their
first enthusiasm have burned out. Interest has turned to
listlessness. Weariness has outstripped well-doing. They
have "passed out" under the combined weight of their fears,
doubts, and daily denials of the One they once professed to
follow. They are no help, but a positive hindrance to the
cause of Christ, not necessarily because they are openly
antagonistic, viciously immoral, or flagrantly corrupt—but
because they have fainted.

As with a physical black out, there are several reasons for
spiritual fainting. Let me briefly mention one or two.

The first is a bad atmosphere: too warm, too stuffy. We've all seen it happen. Even more often, the wrong atmosphere causes us to faint spiritually. Do we pay sufficient attention to the power for good or ill of the atmosphere in which we most often find ourselves? People take on the spiritual coloring of those around them. An individual, a home, or a group can create an atmosphere like a breath of fresh air—sweet, wholesome, and therapeutic to those who go near. There are also atmospheres which are claustrophobic in selfishness or so reek of evil or ill-will that if you stay, you are in grave danger of fainting spiritually.

Weak King Herod didn't want to kill John the Baptist, but he had been too long in a bad atmosphere. He fainted and gave in. Why? "For the sake of them that sat at meat with him." How many who knew better have collapsed into moral unconsciousness because they feared the comments of the "in" crowd, their business associates, their cynically clever friends, their peers? Watch out for the bad atmosphere—it will make you faint.

Some faint at the sight of blood. They can't help it. At the very moment the need for their help is greatest, they are a dead loss in a dead faint.

The rich young ruler had much to offer: enthusiasm, learning, intellect, personality, and serious intent. What an asset to that rough-and-ready band of fishermen this cultured, educated fellow would be! "Come and follow Me," said Jesus after outlining the cost. But the young man was no longer listening. His heart had fainted at the price. The thought of sacrificing what he held most dear cut him to the quick, and he couldn't stand the sight of his own blood. So he "passed out." Yes, and passed out of Christ's sight, useless to the One who could have used him so well. Are we much better? We can add our own private illustrations here. How much sacrifice can we take until we come to the point of passing out?

*
**

What is the spiritual opposite of fainting? The Bible, showing us supreme examples of spiritual stature, declares that their chief characteristic is staying power—a stubborn refusal to faint. The finest thing said of Moses, when he was faced with opposition, disappointment, and heartache, was that he endured. Such staunchness could only be accounted for in terms of God. So they said, "He endured, as seeing Him who is invisible." Paul tells young Timothy, "Endure hardness as a good soldier of Jesus Christ." Jesus says, "He that shall endure to the end, the same shall be saved."

Isaiah sums it up in these tremendous words:

> Hast thou not known? Hast thou not heard that the everlasting God, the Lord, fainteth not neither is weary? He giveth power to the faint and to them that have no might, He increaseth strength. Even the youths shall faint and be weary and the young men shall utterly fall. But they that wait upon the Lord shall renew their strength. They shall mount up with wings as eagles; they shall run and not be weary; and they shall walk and not faint.

The opposite of fainting is endurance; its only source, faith in the unfainting God. "Unless I had believed . . . I had fainted." And it is true.

Life yields no enduring victory over the fears that beset us all, except to faith. Only those who wait on the Lord can be of good courage, for theirs are the hearts He strengthens. So the nub of the psalm is simply this: Without God, our fears deal with us and we faint. With God, we deal with our fears and we endure.

Faint not nor fear, His arm is near;
He changeth not, and thou art dear;
Only believe, and thou shalt see
That Christ is All in all to thee.

"I had fainted," said the Psalmist, "unless I had believed."
And so, friends, will we.

ETERNAL GOD, be with us now. Raise in us new hope as we realize that you alone can keep us from fainting. So increase our faith in Christ who dispels fear and gives us the strength to endure. AMEN.

16

God's very Presence

Joy to Balance

If someone were to ask me what I thought the majority of
worshipers seek when they come to church, I would say,
"Something from God that will not only make up for the
hardnesses, the afflictions, and the sorrows of life, but
balance them out and turn defeated people into victors."

Especially on this day of Communion, we gather with
hidden heartaches, stifled sorrows, bitter burdens, disap-
pointments, and frustrations; wordlessly and hopefully
looking to God to steady, cheer, and empower us. The
words of the Psalmist express this thought exactly, "O Lord
. . . give us joy to balance our affliction for the years when
we knew misfortune"—Psalm 90:15, in a new translation.
"Give us joy to balance . . . our affliction. . . ." This is what
most of us need more than anything else. We need something to compensate for the harshness, the trouble, and the
grief of life. We need a joy to balance. And that is what God
has prepared for us.

Dr. Spooner of Oxford, who was noted for his verbal
mistakes now named "Spoonerisms," used to switch the
first letters of two successive words. He once spoke of "the
tearful chidings of the Gospel" when he meant "the cheerful

tidings. . . ." If we sometimes think that the Sacrament is a matter of tearful chidings and sad rememberings, we're quite wrong. Here are the cheerful tidings of the Gospel; the Good News of what God had done in Christ to redress the power of sin and the grave; to give us joy to balance all the afflictions of life.

It has been suggested that Psalm 90 expresses the prayer of the generation of Israelites who wandered in the wilderness and died without ever entering the Promised Land. It is natural for them to ask God to give them joy to balance the long years of discouragement and wandering. Yet the fulfillment of that joy was not to be theirs, but their successors. We Christians are in a much happier position than they, for the joy God gives is not for some future generation alone, but for us. He will balance our afflictions here and now with His joy.

Some questions. Is there such a joy? If so, what is it like? How do we find it?

*
**

Is there such a joy? Right away there are countless people who would doubt such a thing. They would say:

It's all wishful thinking. You Christians are just foolish—wanting a happy ending to the sordid, miserable story of human life. You want all the wrongs righted; justice done; good triumphant, and evil punished. What a hope! Sure it's desirable—but utterly unrealistic. Joy to balance the sorrow? Peace to balance the pain? Happiness to balance the horror? How very nice. But life's not like that. Don't be so naive, it's just wishful thinking.

So it would be—if we were expecting this joy from the world. The world doesn't give it—for the world doesn't have it—and the world doesn't care. Only God gives it—for only God has it—and only God cares.

We have seen this care and love demonstrated in the life of Jesus for "In all our afflictions, He was afflicted." He bore the weight of our guilt on the Cross though He Himself was sinless. If the Crucifixion had been the end of Jesus, we would never have heard of Him; all His claims would have been proved ultimately false and His truths shown to be lies. We would not be here today, two thousand years after Christ's earthly life, asking God for joy to balance our afflictions, for there would be no certainty that God, if He existed, even cared. But through Christ, we know that God does care. Not only that, He cares sufficiently to vindicate righteousness, truth, goodness, and love. God balances out the Cross with the Resurrection, the volume of sin with the vastness of His forgiveness. He outweighs death with life, hate with love, evil with goodness, sorrow with joy.

In Jesus, the scales tip with a tremendous thump to the side of eternal good. We know that there is a joy to balance; a joy God has given in Christ, through the vindication of His life, to those who trust Him.

*
**

What distinguishes this joy from the joy the world offers—which most people seek? There are certain differences.

The first is that the world's joy is haphazard—a matter of chance. As Robert Burns puts it:

> Pleasures are like poppies spread,
> You seize the flow'r, its bloom is shed;
> Or like the snowfall in the river,
> A moment white—then melts forever.

The world's joys and pleasures are spread with as little thought and purpose behind their distribution as that. Worldly joy is not linked to a person's worth or deserving, for someone who has had an easy life may be full of it. Nor does it depend upon character. In Psalm 37:35 the writer complains, "I have seen the wicked in great power, spreading himself like a green bay tree." The world's joy is a haphazard thing—not a joy to balance life's sorrows. With no such purpose behind it, there is no justice in it.

Moreover, if the world's joy contains no justice, it has no permanence. I quoted the Psalmist about the wicked flourishing like a green bay tree. The next verse continues, "Yet he passed away, and lo, he was not; yea, I sought him, but he could not be found." One year, all joy; the next, all gone. Poor, sad Lord Byron wasn't very old when he wrote:

> There's not a joy the world can give
>   Like that it takes away,
> When the glow of early thought declines
>   In feeling's dull decay.

If one thing is sure, it is that the world's joy is very vulnerable, at the mercy of the activities and actions of others. A change of circumstance or a different outlook, and it is gone; a transient joy affected by circumstance rather than a balancing joy which affects circumstance.

The world's joy is haphazard—there is no justice in it. The world's joy is fleeting—there is no permanence in it. The third fact: the world's joy is incomplete. Most people discover sooner or later as a fact of experience that even in life's greatest joys, there is an element of incompleteness. As we say in Scotland, "There's aye a something." In the best scene, there's aye a something. Nothing is ever completely perfect and unalloyed. It may be the lingering of some regret or some incident that spoils our happiness.

Even the dim thought in the back of the mind that this is too good to last can mar its perfection. Adelaide Anne Procter, a hymnwriter of the last century, uses this feeling as a guide to the greater joy God gives—perfect and complete.

> I thank Thee more that all our joy
>   Is touched with pain;
> That shadows fall on brightest hours,
>   That thorns remain;
> So that earth's bliss may be our guide,
>   And not our chain.

Were earth's joy complete, we would feel no need for anything more. But it isn't complete, and so we look to God for what He alone can give. What God gives to balance our afflictions is unlike the joy the world gives. It is different in three basic ways.

First, it is not haphazard. Nobody gets it by chance, but by character. There is a justice in God's joy which accounts for the fact that truly good people, faced by overwhelming odds, are not swept off their feet but can maintain a cheerful equilibrium. Second, it is not a transient condition, a passing uplift that is affected by circumstance. On the contrary, it affects circumstance, for there is a permanence in God's joy. And third, it is not incomplete like the joys of the world. There is perfection in the joy of God, because something of God Himself is in it. This exuberance springs from a dependence on His abundant resources.

Just. Permanent. Complete. Such is the joy that God gives us to balance our tears and troubles.

*
**

How am I so sure that this is a true picture of the joy God gives? In Christ's farewell talk to His disciples just

before His betrayal, the thought of bequeathing them His
joy is foremost in His mind.

In John 15, Jesus is speaking to His followers on the need
to dwell in His love and heed His commands. In verse 11,
He goes on to say, "I have spoken thus to you, so that I
may have joy in you and your joy may be complete." Just as
we know that our gladness is greatly increased if a loved
one—a parent maybe—is pleased by the way we are living
and justly proud of us, so too do we experience something
of the complete joy God gives when we know that Jesus
delights in us. If He rejoices in us because we are dwelling
in His love and obeying His words, then He promises us a
joy that reflects His good pleasure; unalloyed, perfect, and
complete.

You can see how this is bound to work. As long as we are
doing His will, we know His joy. When we start doing our
will, we lose it. We find happiness in His approval as we
seek to obey His commands. When He rejoices in us, then
our joy is complete. But if our living is such that He cannot
bless it, then we also lose the joy He offers. Ask yourself,
"Can Christ rejoice in the way I live?" If He cannot, don't
expect anything to balance your afflictions, for His joy is
not haphazard. There is a justice in it. It is not for the
person who ignores His word.

There is joy in His approval; just and complete. But
furthermore, there is joy in His Presence. Jesus has been
telling his disciples He must soon leave them. They are
filled with sadness at the prospect. Then He says: "For the
moment you are sad at heart, but I shall see you again.
Then you will be joyful and no one shall rob you of your
joy." Here, He promises something that cannot be taken
away, a joy that is permanent and secure. What is its source?
Simply the fact that He will be with them again. They will
not be left comfortless and forsaken (the very thing they
dread), for His Presence will be their constant delight.

In the last analysis, we can never have God's balancing joy neatly wrapped up in a convenient package; it is part and parcel of His Presence. We cannot have it without Him. Indeed, God Himself is the only permanent bliss that can possibly balance out all the afflictions of life. He alone can affect our circumstances and remain unaffected by them. His Presence is the determining factor.

Hans Lilje, who later became the Bishop of Hannover, was a prisoner of the Gestapo. In his book, *The Valley of the Shadow*, he tells of a celebration of the Sacrament one Christmas Eve in a Berlin prison. This was possible due to the humaneness of the commandant who, for this very reason, was soon relieved of his post. The three prisoners who took part in this Communion were all under the threat of death. This is how the survivor describes it:

> It was a very quiet celebration of the Sacrament, full of deep confidence in God. Almost palpably, the wings of the Divine Mercy hovered over us. We were prisoners in the power of the Gestapo, in Berlin. But the peace of God enfolded us. It was real and present . . . and I praised God from my whole heart!

Only God can prepare a joyous feast for us in the midst of enemies; in the face of sorrows; in the place of suffering. Our joy is Jesus.

> Jesus, Thou Joy of loving hearts,
>   Thou Fount of life, Thou Light of men,
> From the best bliss that earth imparts
>   We turn unfilled to Thee again.

O LORD, give us Thyself. Be Thou the Joy to balance our circumstances, our sorrows, and our sin. Be near to each one of us. As we seek to do your will from this day forward, so may we know the bliss which is your Presence. Through Christ. AMEN.

17

The extraordinary in the ordinary

Surprise, Surprise!

On October 7, 1952, I was ordained to the Christian Ministry in my first church. That milestone event in my life occurred in a bonnie country church in the southwest of Scotland. As a new minister with no record, it was the only church for which I ever applied. At the installation, the old minister who had labored in the neighboring parish for thirty-seven years preached from the text, "And Jesus went on to another village. . . ." As I sat and listened, not in my wildest dreams did I imagine that I would ever stand in the pulpit of the Georgetown Presbyterian Church in Washington, D.C.

If I've learned one thing in life, it is that we worship a God who ever surprises us. For the Christian, the most ordinary occasion, the commonplace duty, the everyday task faithfully done, is the locus from which something of startling wonder may emerge. This is the way God works—the extraordinary in the ordinary.

Surprise, surprise! The Holy Child—in a manger. Messiah—from backwater Bethlehem. The world's greatest Teacher—from a carpenter's bench. The Son of God—on a wooden cross. An empty tomb—after the burial. No wonder true Christians in every age have never found life dull. God's next surprise could be anywhere even in the most familiar situation.

*
* *

Acts 3 begins in a very commonplace way, "One day at three in the afternoon, the hour of prayer, Peter and John were on their way up to the temple." The ordinary beginning that preceded an amazing end.

"One day at three in the afternoon. . . ." For the devout Jew, 9:00 A.M., 12:00 noon, and 3:00 P.M. were the times of prayer. And it was felt doubly precious if one could offer these prayers actually in the temple courts. So although Peter and John had come to a new faith, they did not disregard the old discipline of worship. Indeed, their new understanding deepened the meaning of old traditions; just as the reverence and respect enjoined by the Ten Commandments is not canceled, but positively endorsed by Christ's command to love God and one's neighbor as oneself.

These two disciples did not set out with the intention of taking part in some amazing event. Worship was their habit. They were doing what they usually did, as was the second character in the story, the lame man. If you had asked him his plans for that hot afternoon, he would have told you it would be the same old routine: carried to a familiar spot, dumped there, and left to beg the whole day through. The charity of others was his livelihood. Never did he dream of that particular day being any different. And neither did the third group in the story—the people already worshiping in the temple—earnest, dutiful folk most of them. When they went to the House of God that day, never did they think of the bombshell of praise that would be hurled into their midst in the shape of a cured cripple.

So there they were, three sets of people about their usual

business. We may well see ourselves in one or another of these three categories.

*
**

There was the beggar. He was a beggar because he was disabled from birth. He couldn't carry a load to earn his livelihood. Indeed, he was a burden to others. As the narrative says, he used to be carried every day and laid at the gate of the temple called Beautiful to beg from the people as they went in.

This man had a physical defect, which meant he had to be carried. There are multitudes with character defects, spiritual inadequates who have to have the very same thing done for them. Some are crippled by a constricting bad habit. They are hooked on hopelessness. They are handicapped by past failures, paralyzed by fear, and rendered immobile by the weakness of their will. Whatever the cause, they have to be carried. They are the leaners, not the lifters.

So here we have the lame beggar, symbol of all the other inadequates who have to be carried. Notice where he was taken—to the door of the temple, just outside the House of God. It is not accidental that time and again, the love of God and love of mankind go hand in hand. Remember, Christ condemned much of the formalized religion of the Jewish Church of His day, yet even so, this beggar knew that it was at the door of the church that he would have his best chance. Those in need do not look with the greatest certainty to frequenters of casinos, liquor stores, or night spots. Their best bet for help still lies among those moved by the Spirit of Christ.

What was the crippled man looking for? Like many another inadequate he sought something equally insufficient, a handout. Something that at the end of the day would leave him exactly as he was. As the proverb says,

"Better to teach a man to fish, than to give a man a fish."
This is precisely the difference between the handout and
the hand up. The beggar was looking for a handout. Peter
and John offered him a hand up. And when he took it, this
lame man was surprised by the joy of healing.

I am not going to rationalize or analyze this miracle.
With God all things are possible. And if in the name of
Christ, in the name of love, you stretch out a hand to give
another a lift, you will be astonished at what love can do.
The trouble is that many want only the handout and not
the hand up. For the hand up means contact. It means a
relationship, and such people don't want to be changed.
Help on their terms or not at all! So, of course, they remain
as they are—inadequate, never surprised by the joy of being
made whole.

None of us is ever made whole on our own terms; only
on God's terms. And that means accepting the proffered
hand up from Christ as we realize how much we need it.
"One day, about three in the afternoon, Peter and John
were on their way up to the temple. . . ." And what
happened? The handicapped man at the gate begged for
charity. We read that Peter fixed his eyes on him and said,
"I have no silver or gold, but what I have I give you."

*
**

If the cripple was surprised by being healed, the apostles
were surprised at the outcome of their giving. There is so
much more to giving than the gift. Laurens Van der Post
tells of the ending of Dutch colonial rule in Indonesia and
of how the departing governor said to him with a sense of
hurt, "I cannot understand it! Look what we have done for
them. Look at the schools and the hospitals we have given
them. We've done away with malaria, plague, and dysentery.
Look at the roads, the railway, and the industries—yet they

want us to go. Can you tell me why?" And Van der Post replied simply, "Yes, I think I can. I'm afraid it is because you never had the right look in your eyes when you spoke to them."

I am sure that when Peter and John fixed their eyes on that beggar, he saw in them the right look: a focus of real attention, genuine interest, true care; no impersonal or patronizing glance. Like their Lord, these men spoke to crowds but had learned never to lose the individual in the mass. They looked on this man with such concentrated compassion that he knew they believed him a creature of worth. He felt himself in the presence of men who cared. They had the right look in their eyes; stirring his hope, quickening his faith in human nature, before they ever spoke. Peter then said something that may not sound very dramatic, but yet is the greatest offer of help anyone can make. He said, "Such as I have, give I thee."

That is the best anybody can ever do. And yet it is also the least we can do, and be Christian. Is our giving to others in time, effort, and money always up to the limit of such as we have? Or is it a case of "Such as suits me, give I thee"? If our standard is the lesser one, we shall never be surprised by the joy of giving which is only for those like Peter and John who gave as Christ gave. Indeed, they passed on their greatest possession—the love of Christ.

To know Christ is to love Christ. To love Christ is to want to give like Christ. And to give like Christ is to be surprised at what such giving does. For, like Shakespeare's mercy,

> It blesseth him that gives and him that takes:
> 'Tis mightiest in the mightiest; it becomes
> The throned monarch better than his crown; . . .

Friends, have we ever been surprised by such a joy of giving?
"One day about three in the afternoon, the hour of

prayer, Peter and John were on their way up to the temple."
The manner in which those disciples lived and acted outside
the temple eventually made all the difference to the worship
inside. And this is always true. For our words and deeds
and thoughts outside the church have an uncanny way of
adding to, or subtracting from, the reality and effectiveness
of the worship inside.

*
**

This consideration brings us to the last group of people
in our story, the worshipers in the temple. We could call
them the folk in the pews.

Someone has written, "When my father went to church
and sat in his pew, he felt he was doing enough." No doubt
many think the same. Yet even for such people, God has a
surprise in store. Just when they think it's the old routine—
Surprise, Surprise! Some hymn of praise, some word of
power, some familiar face that shines with new hope, some
voice that sings with certainty, or a cry of thanksgiving and
the whole atmosphere is suddenly changed.

That's what happened one day in the temple. The lame
man was healed not only physically but spiritually. For we
read, "He entered with them, walking and leaping and
praising God." And because of his presence instead of it
being just another meeting, it was the most exciting thing
that had ever happened to those worshipers. We are told
they were filled with wonder and amazement, and many
who heard Peter's subsequent message became believers.

There they were surprised by God, filled with wonder
and belief. And notice what caused it—a cured cripple's
shout of praise. No worship can ever be tame and dull if in
it there is some wasted soul, some bowed-down character,
some moral inadequate whom Christ has just raised to

newness of life. And goodness knows—God knows—it could even be us. For still:

> He speaks; and, listening to His voice,
>   New life the dead receive,
> The mournful broken hearts rejoice,
>   The humble poor believe.

> Here Him, ye deaf; His praise, ye dumb,
>   Your loosened tongues employ;
> Ye blind, behold your Saviour come;
>   And leap, ye lame, for joy!

"One day, Peter and John were on their way up to the temple." And lives were changed. God grant us also such joyful surprise as we worship Him now.

———————————

ALMIGHTY GOD, ever ready to surprise us, make us aware and alert. Make us ready to receive you as we experience your power in us—healing; your power in us—prompting us to give; your power in us—prompting us to wonder and faith and joy. Through Christ we ask it. AMEN.

V

Throughout the Year

18

The New Year

The Time of Our Lives

"We had the time of our lives," people say. "One assumes they had a great vacation or a really wonderful New Year's party. But listen:

> Seventy years is all we have—
>   eighty years if we are strong;
> Yet all they bring us are trouble and sorrow;
>   life is soon over and we are gone.

Such is the Psalmist's definition of "time of our lives." A dose of reality therapy for a new year. Hardly a party! Yet, as we all know, reality does contain cause for celebration, as well as sacrifice; time for laughter, as well as loss.

Each of us has this one time to live, this brief period which we can fill with what we will; within which we can use our particular gifts, abilities, and opportunities for what we choose.

At age eighty, Dr. David Read, the long-serving, outstanding Scots minister of New York's Madison Avenue Presbyterian Church, preached his final sermon. Someone who was there told me that Dr. Read said that over the decades he had preached many thousands of sermons which, like this last one, would doubtless be forgotten. But as a postscript to them all, he had one thing for his congregation to remember: God loves *you*.

How will each of us spend the time of our lives? What will its theme be? Will it leave a simple, memorable postscript? How will we live? Will we live for pleasure, personal profit, or status? Will we live for sensuality, excitement, or Mankind's good? Or will we live for God's glory? These are a few of the many ways in which the time of our lives can be spent.

***

I know that no motive is pure and unalloyed—even the best motives have traces of selfishness. In our lives, one motive will emerge stronger than the rest. Is that motive focused on self, on others, or on God? All of us leave a message—a message of faith, fear, or frustration; either one that encourages, or one that produces greater hopelessness.

Many years ago, long before the current drug scene, the twenty-year-old grandson of former British prime minister Harold Macmillan committed suicide. The young man had known every advantage of birth, position, and education, yet he was a slave to drugs, to which he had been introduced by "a friend." The family doctor told the coroner that there was no serious illness; he was highly intelligent and was always after something to stimulate him. "This was the whole pattern of his existence—somewhat unstable, and sort of groping for facts in life generally." Note this phrase, "Groping for facts in life generally." To how many does that apply right now?

Surely one fact of life that should guide us on how to live is the fact of its briefness—short enough without deliberately cutting it shorter. It may seem obvious to say, "Life is short," but there is profound implication in that phrase. If Psalm 90 gives us the span of our time, then Job 7:6 gives us the speed of our time. Job says, "My days are swifter than a weaver's shuttle. . . ."

The vivid figure of speech tells anyone who has ever watched a weaver at the loom that this is what life is like. As the shuttle bearing the thread (the woof) flashes backwards and forwards between the cross threads (the warp), so our days flash past—morning to evening, evening to morning—faster even, says Job, than the weaver's shuttle. What does this vibrant picture tell us about living the time of our lives?

*
**

The obvious point of comparison between our lives and the weaver's shuttle is speed: the swiftness with which our days go by and the swiftness with which the shuttle flies. This truth makes little impression on the young. To those with all life ahead, time drags waiting for next Christmas. Only as one grows older is the speed of time better appreciated. The older you become, the faster it seems to go. Yet the lesson of the flying shuttle is not simply that time flies. (Time flies for all, whether people realize it or not.) The lesson lies in our asking how well our time is filled. Has the best been put into it? Or are the flashing days cluttered with trivialities, half-finished attempts, botched opportunities, and the careless waste of precious hours?

The weaver's shuttle is not only swift, but accurate as it moves back and forth carrying the yarn with it. With each flashing pass, it fulfills its function. Though it speeds, it performs its task. A racing shuttle with no woof left behind in the warp is futile. Yet that is the picture of so many lives: all speed, rush, stimuli, but nothing of worth left to show for it—nothing done well. Such people resemble mad touch-typists going at great speed, yet whose accuracy is so faulty that the resulting pages are nonsense. Life may be swift, but that is no reason to make it meaningless. As the old mission hymn puts it:

> Give to each flying minute
> Something to keep in store;
> Work, for the night is coming,
> When one works no more.

The first lesson of the weaver's shuttle: Do it *well*. For the day will come when you and I will stop. We will lay down the tools of our trade, the end of our attempt at earthly living. No more touching up botched work. No more going back to lift life's dropped stitches. No further chance to delete our mistakes on time's computers. Such as it is, your record and mine will have to stand as we leave them when Death comes to the door. So don't let all your plans for goodness, love, and service wait for another occasion in more suitable surroundings. Don't let this day's work and worship, compassion and companionship go by unconsidered. Do whatever you are working at now as well as you can, for you can never relive this day.

That is one reason for "doing it well." Another is this. Paul said to the Colossians, "Whatever ye do, do it heartily as to the Lord." The New English Bible translates this, "Put your whole heart into it, as if you were doing it for the Lord." We do it well not merely because time is limited; we do it well for a Master. To each one of us in our different daily tasks comes this call which transforms duty into delight: we do it well because we do it for Him. Days may be swifter than a weaver's shuttle; nevertheless, do well whatever comes within their scope.

*
**

The second lesson of the weaver's shuttle: If in this life we do it well, we must also do it *now*. Do the good now! The swiftly traveling shuttle carries with it a specific length of thread which, like life itself, will run out at some point. Our time shuttle carries with it a definite amount of weeks, months, and years.

My first parish was a rural community near Lockerbie in Scotland, where the church was surrounded by a graveyard. One particular stone had been put up with a man's name along with his date of birth engraved on it. There was no date of death because it had not yet taken place. The man had erected the gravestone to himself, possibly because he didn't think anyone else would. Obviously he didn't know the second date. Not one of us knows our own second date.

The fact that we do not know the length of our thread of life is often an excuse for not "doing it now." To think we are bound to have more time to do that kindness or make up with so-and-so or speak the appreciative word—there's no "bound to" about it. An incalculable amount of misery, suffering, and remorse is directly the result of not doing the right thing now, and putting off the God-given noble impulse or generous purpose until some other time. Why would God have given us that good impulse unless He had meant us to act on it?

If all the kind letters had been written when first thought of, how many lonely souls would have been cheered? If the friendly visit had been paid when it was first thought of, it might have made all the difference to that relationship. Never suppose that you can make up with a neglected friend by visiting them in the hospital. Repent on your own deathbed if you like, but not on someone else's! If in the present, we fail to do certain good things, the chances are we will never do them. Postpone evil, but never good.

Patience Strong has a verse about the way people act

when someone dies—flowers are sent and notes written.
She goes on:

> Their good points we remember; their failings we
>   ignore.
> We wish that we'd been nicer, and done a little more.
> We speak of them with kindness and loving things are
>   said . . .
> But isn't it a pity we wait until they're dead?

It's more than a pity, it's a tragedy—this folly of not doing
good now and being too late forever.

So if there is a kind purpose in your heart for a living
soul, express it now. If you're thinking of beginning a
better way of life this year, begin it now. If you propose to
end your days a loyal servant of Christ, then volunteer now.
For *now* is the day of salvation. We all have so much time—
we don't know how long. Use it now before we reach the
end of the line on the weaver's swift shuttle of life. So
whatever it is, great or small, that will make you a better
person, benefit others, and glorify God; whatever impulse
is in your heart for right—do it now.

Job says, "My days are swifter than a weaver's shuttle."
Therefore let them pass not only with speed, but with
accuracy—do it well! Therefore value their time and use it
for good—do it now!

*
**

The last lesson of the weaver's shuttle: Realize that your
individual piece of the pattern is part of a larger design so
that in all you do, do it for the future, beyond death. Do it
for eternity.

This is a matter of right perspective. Although you have
only this "time of your life" which moves swifter than a

weaver's shuttle, you can use it not only to brighten the present, but also to shape the future through your influence on others in ways you could not possibly imagine. You have now the opportunity to make your own personal contribution to God's pattern—His working out of all things.

At memorial services, I often use the second verse of a poem entitled "The Weaver" which I learned as a boy. The author is unknown except to God, who alone knows how many have been helped by these words:

My life is but a weaving
Between my Lord and me,
I cannot choose the colors
He worketh steadily.
Ofttimes He weaveth sorrow,
And I, in foolish pride,
Forget He sees the upper
And I, the underside.

Not till the loom is silent
And the shuttles cease to fly,
Shall God unroll the canvas
And explain the reason why
The dark threads are as needful
In the Weaver's skillful hand,
As the threads of gold and silver
In the pattern He has planned.

"Not till the loom is silent." We cannot judge a great woven design by a portion, but only by the finished product. And this is the Christian interpretation of life—that whatever we do now, be the threads we handle dark or bright, we do for eternity. Handling the somber as well as the shining is all part of the pattern. *Now* is the start of the way we shall be—bad or good, cowardly or courageous, a lost wanderer or a child coming home to God. This time of our life is not an unfinished, meaningless fragment of weal or woe, but part of the pattern of eternity.

We don't get this perspective from Job. He says, "My days are swifter than a weaver's shuttle and spent without hope." We don't get it from the Psalmist, who says, "Life is soon over and we are gone." Where do we get our confidence? From the Resurrection of Christ. Paul speaks of the victory we have through Christ which opens up new vistas, not only upon the future, but upon the present. He says in the last verse of 1 Corinthians 15:

Therefore, my beloved, work for the Lord always. Work without limit, since you know that in the Lord, your labor cannot be lost.

For the Christian, life is not a broken column, a half-finished story, an unrealized dream, an incomplete circle. In God is fullness, wholeness, completeness. In the Lord nothing of worth, nothing of truth, nothing of goodness and right is ever in vain. All the pieces fit.

John describes how at the Last Supper the disciples are squabbling about who is the greatest, "And Jesus, knowing that He was come from God, and went to God . . ." (from God . . . to God, the complete circle), "took a towel and washed the disciples' feet."

Even the most lowly, ordinary act has a new significance when we see it as part of the whole pattern. The Christian's greatness lies not in the length of days or in doing great things, but in doing all things faithfully "as unto the Lord" against the background of God and in the perspective of eternity.

Like Christ, we too are come from God and go to God. However swift the weaver's shuttle of this mortality may fly, the way in which we handle life, even at its most hard or humdrum, is of eternal significance and worth. Even if, like Job, our days are swifter than a weaver's shuttle, nevertheless we shall remain confident, with Paul, that our labor in the Lord cannot—*cannot*—be lost.

May we live the Christian life in this year by doing it well, doing good now, and doing all things for eternity. Then we will have—here—the time of our lives.

ALMIGHTY GOD, who has given us this chance at life, forgive us as we have botched it and failed in the past. The great Good News is that you do love us and are ever ready to give us another chance if we seek your help, guidance, and forgiveness. We do that now, praying that from this day on we may use the time of our lives in ways which will please you, bless others, and build up our own souls for your Presence. Hear this our prayer through Christ. AMEN.

19

Tomorrow is in our hands today

The Peace We Seek

In the course of the 1990–1991 crisis in the Persian Gulf, I came across the views of many Church leaders. Their views led me to the conclusion that they live in what I would call an "if only" world.

The need to fight Hitler would never have arisen, said one, if only the Allies had not treated Germany the way they did after World War I. A Hitler then would never have happened. So presumably neither would have Napoleon nor Attila the Hun. In other words, circumstances produce bad people—a dubious theory. Says another, "If only sanctions had been given time to work." What fuzzy thinking! As if a proven callous leader would eventually yield, being touched by the sight of his besieged, starving citizens. For that is what real sanctions mean—siege. As if slow death were morally superior to quick!

As the U.N. deadline for Saddam Hussein's withdrawal from Kuwait approached, the National Council of Churches organized a message to President Bush from thirty-two Protestant leaders pleading, "Do not lead our nation into this abyss." For once begun, "it is unlikely that this battle can be contained in either scope, intensity, or time." In fact it was contained in all three. Once again these so-called leaders were wrong. Besides which, none of Saddam's actions—initial aggression, murder, torture—merited a moral mention from the Council. A group of Czechoslovakian Christians said of the Council's stance: "Your church representatives have underestimated the criminal nature of the Marxist regimes. Now they underestimate the criminal nature of Saddam Hussein. Consequently we do not trust your church representatives." Quite so!

Through all these views runs the recurrent theme "if only." "War could have been prevented if only we had had enough foresight." War could have been prevented "if only we were prepared to talk forever while halfheartedly tightening other screws." War can be prevented "if only you listen to us," says the National Council of Churches, which has lost the power to discriminate.

All of them forget one basic fact; we do not live in an "if only" world where people are unselfishly wise, individuals sweetly reasonable, and moral leaders indubitably right. We live in an "as is" world. Like that corner of the furniture store where they've gathered all the shop-soiled items: the broken, chipped, scratched, dented, and incomplete. They are only available, as the sign says, "as is!"

This is our world. The reality of sin runs through it. All who exhibit a natural desire for peace had better be very clear about the intransigent nature of human sin in the whole scheme of things, and realize that many choices are not clear-cut between good and evil, but are between greater and lesser evils. This is the world as it is: the background to any peace we seek.

*
**

Peace in our day is the hope of every generation. The parent, the child, the loved one, the worker, the owner—all have much to lose and greatly desire peace in their time. This seems reasonable enough, but the trouble is that this desire is often basically selfish. For while one generation may achieve "peace in their time," their way of doing it may only be storing up aggression farther down the road and for their children's children.

It is not enough to say, "Oh if only people weren't like that!" Let us see what we can do to prevent the peace we seek from being a replay of the past.

To this end here is a text from 2 Kings 20:19:

Then said Hezekiah to Isaiah, "Good is the word of the Lord which thou hast spoken." And Hezekiah said, "Is it not good if peace and security be in my days?"

Here is the story behind the text, a thumbnail sketch of human nature very like our own.

Hezekiah, king of Judah, was a good king. We are told he did that which was right in the eyes of the Lord. Moreover, he rebelled against the king of Assyria resulting in the eventual siege of Jerusalem by the Assyrians. But through God's intervention the city was not taken. Later, Hezekiah was dangerously ill, but after a desperate prayer to God, he recovered. It was just at this time that there came to his court envoys from the court of Babylon. (Where was Babylon? Sixty miles south of Baghdad!) They brought letters and a present because they had heard of his illness. Hezekiah was pleased by this visit. He liked being made much of by a great foreign power. He proudly showed the Babylonian visitors his entire palace—his armory, his treasure rooms, his vaults—they saw them all.

It was then that Isaiah the prophet came upon the scene, and watching the departing envoys said:

"Where did these men come from?"

"Babylon," said Hezekiah.

"How much have they seen of your palace?"

"More or less everything," answered Hezekiah.

"Then hear the Word of the Lord," said Isaiah. "The day is coming when all that is in your house, all that your forebears have laid up in store, everything, shall be carried away into Babylon and nothing left. And even your sons, they shall be taken away to the palace of the king of Babylon."

Then said Hezekiah, "Good is the word of the Lord which thou hast spoken." And then he added (possibly under his breath as if talking to himself), "Is it not good if peace and security be in my days?"

In other words, Hezekiah realized that it could well happen as Isaiah had said, and that his children's children could be slaves in Babylon as a result of his showing off his treasures, whetting the Babylonians' greed. Nevertheless, he felt by then *he* would be well out of it. It was good enough for him that there would be peace in his time. "Is it not good," he said, "if peace and security be in my days?"

Peace in my days. This is the profound desire of the majority. Must it always be a selfish desire like that of Hezekiah? Or can we seek peace in the present in such a way as will keep peace in the future?

What is the price of an unselfish peace in our days? Look at it like this. As nations and as individuals there are three days that must concern us all: our yesterday, our today, and our tomorrow. There can be no true peace that does not take all three into account. Hezekiah's life, like ours, had its yesterday, its today, and its tomorrow. I want us to use that life as a guide that we may learn from his mistakes, and so seek an unselfish peace in our days.

*
**

Look at yesterday.

Hezekiah's yesterday was very like ours. When Hezekiah looked back, he remembered with thanks what had been done for him. He had been delivered from the oppression of the conqueror. His home had been spared. His life had been spared. He looked back and he gave thanks to God for the deliverance in his yesterday.

As one who clearly remembers the bombings of World War II and taking refuge under the stairs when the bombers flew over, I have no doubt that the miasma of Hitler would not have stopped with complete conquest in Europe, anymore than the sun of Japan arose merely to shine on the western rim of the Pacific. Should it be casually dismissed—being delivered and spared? Other lives were not spared: people who looked forward to a home of their own and children, in a tomorrow they would never see.

The inscription on the memorial to the men who fell in 1944 in the Battle of Kohima in Burma expresses in four short lines the immensity of the sacrifice, the sorrow, the pain, the loss. It reads:

> When you go home,
> Tell them of us,
> And say, "For your tomorrow
> We gave today."

They gave the most they could give. They gave their present and their future for our present and our future.

No one can give us a ready-made new world order, but all such sacrifice can and does give us a new chance. If we have spoiled by thoughtless, selfish living the gift of tomorrow given by others, the blame is ours not theirs.

We have been given a new chance by so many people—

those who died or were maimed in war and those like
Madame Curie who laid down their lives in peace. She died,
you remember, from blood cancer, the effect from the rays
of the radium she had discovered and was processing. While
she could have made a personal fortune from her discoveries, she would not patent a single one. For a sick mankind's
tomorrow she gave her today.

Remember, too, there was One of whom it was said as
He hung on the Cross, "He saved others, Himself He could
not save." But that gibe was a lie. He saved others, Himself
He *would* not save. There, God, in Love, gave Himself, that
there might be a tomorrow of new chance for sinful men
and women.

How can we hope for real peace in our world or in our
hearts unless we are constantly prepared to remember with
thanks the deliverance of yesterday? There would be little
opportunity for people to go out and protest about rights
if the past sacrifice hadn't given them the chance to do so.
Not only should we thank God for what people have done
for us, but for what He has done for us in Christ.

*
**

Peace in our days must begin with thankful remember-
ance of yesterday. But more, it has to do with today.

Hezekiah's today was a prosperous today. Hezekiah, we
read, showed the Babylonian envoys "all the house of his
precious things, the silver, the gold, the spices, the precious
ointment and all the house of his armor and all that was
found of his treasures: there was nothing in his house, nor
in all his dominion that Hezekiah showed them not." I'm
afraid he was a bit of a show-off.

What was he bragging about? A lot of nonessentials:
luxuries, spices, ointment, gold, silver, jewels, wealth. These
were his treasures, and they are very like the modern world's

treasures—a lot of things which people are made to feel are essential to happiness and without which they will be left unfulfilled and forever dissatisfied. They end up telling themselves that luxuries are really necessities and that prosperity is life's purpose.

The corollary is this: For many individuals and through them for many business enterprises, the only thing that counts is the bottom line. Maximum profit! Would Saddam Hussein have been so well armed had a different consideration played a part? Unless we have a bigger goal than money, unbridled capitalism will lead to a dead end of its own devising, just as communism did in its own way.

For the one basic, often neglected factor that runs through all ideologies is self-willed, unregenerate human nature. Once a Russian soldier said to an American, "We communists are happy, not because we are rich but because we know where we are going." A goal! As it turned out, they didn't! We in the West had better know where we're going—and something better than the bottom line too—or we will end in history's rubbish dump.

What we need is a "culture of character." That phrase comes from a recent speech by Health and Human Services Secretary Louis W. Sullivan. He said this:

> At the Department of Health and Human Services, we are called upon to address some of our nation's most urgent problems, ranging from infant mortality, to drug abuse, to the AIDS epidemic, to teen pregnancy, to the disproportionately poor health and excess mortality affecting America's minority citizens. And it has become ever more clear to me that, all too often, these problems arise precisely from an erosion of basic values, and from the collapse of the institutions that teach them. . . .

He called on all Americans to create a new "culture of character" and reaffirm "values like self-discipline, integrity, taking responsibility for one's acts, respect for others, perseverance, moderation, and a commitment to serve others and the broader community." Study after study has shown, he said, "that children who are raised in an environment of strong values . . . are less likely to be trapped in drug addiction, less likely to become involved in crime, to become teen parents, or to commit suicide."

Responding to charges that emphasizing values is tantamount to "blaming the victim" who is disadvantaged by poverty, disease, drug abuse, or lack of opportunity, he said:

> The tragic truth is that the language of "victimization" is the true victimizer—a great crippler of young minds and spirits. I would go so far as to say that those who refuse to talk about personal behavior and the factors we can control, and insist instead that we focus on what we cannot control, are in effect *laming* the victim. (italics mine)

Well said! It is easy to blame things over which we have no personal control—the folly of the past, the sin of the system, the failure of society. It's a very different matter and much more vital to take responsibility for the way in which we choose to live and the effects those choices have upon others.

For the sin of systems is the sin of individuals writ large. Hezekiah's grandchildren would not have needed to end in slavery had he been able to control his personal desire to show off, to declare the greatness of his treasure! If human pride and self-will are not checked, and the goals for living are not reassessed in favor of responsibility and righteousness as children of a loving God, then the peace we seek will have no firm foundation in the human heart. If it is not founded there, it will not happen.

*
**

Peace in our days begins with a thankful remembrance of yesterday. It continues with a clear reevaluation of today. And it proceeds to a rededication for tomorrow. This is where Hezekiah failed. He didn't seem to care what would happen in the tomorrow. At least there would be peace in his day.

Today fashions tomorrow, just as yesterday molded today. The Quaker's motto "It is better to light a candle than to curse the darkness" should be ours. We Christians must do exactly that for the future. If the future is unknown, we need not let it remain dark for our children and their children. Because we have a light in Christ which if we kindle today—in our lives, in our homes, among our families, in our church, in our community, in our world—will brighten and guide the generations of tomorrow.

The only unselfish peace we can seek in our day is that which produces the rededication of our life for tomorrow. Don't let anyone tell you that one life, here and there, doesn't really matter against the vastness of the world scene. For it is through dedicated individuals, one by one, that God has always worked. The only thing that determines the extent of His effect through us is the measure of our dedication to Him.

Well, there it is. Tomorrow is in our hands today.

You may know the fable about the boy who devised the scheme by which he would trick a wise old man. Catching a small bird in a snare, then holding it concealed but alive in his hand, he would ask the old man, "Is this bird alive or dead?" If the wise man said it was alive, the boy would give his hand a quick squeeze and then show the bird dead. If he said dead, the boy would simply open his hand and let the bird fly away. So whatever answer he gave, the wise man would be proved wrong. With the live bird in his hand the boy came with his question, "Mr. Wise Man, is this bird dead or is it alive?" The old man did not look at the boy's hand. Instead he looked full into the boy's eyes and said quietly, "My son, it is whatever you want it to be."

Whatever you want it to be. Friends, we have in our hands that part of the future bound up with our influence upon home, family, children, friends, and colleagues. For good or ill, we today are imperceptibly fashioning their tomorrow by the cumulative thoughts, words, and deeds over which we have control.

What will tomorrow be? Listen. God is saying to each of us, "It is whatever *you* want it to be." The onus is on us—in the face of life and death itself—still to be steadying and vital examples of the faith that knows:

God is our refuge and strength, a very present help in time of trouble. Therefore will not we fear. . . .

There can be no true peace in our days that does not begin with thankful remembrance of yesterday, continue with a clear reevaluation of today, and end with a personal rededication for tomorrow.

Is this the peace *we* seek?

———————

ALMIGHTY GOD, when decisions are difficult and choices not clear-cut, help us to decide aright as we see them in the context of our gratitude for yesterday, our responsibility for today, and our dedication for tomorrow. Thus in your Presence we would seek the source of our peace and the world's. Through Christ we pray. AMEN.

20

Stewardship

Insight on Dedication

"Four score and seven years ago, our fathers brought forth upon this continent a new nation." So begins that brief, well-known address that Abraham Lincoln delivered in Gettysburg. At that cemetery in Pennsylvania, Lincoln spoke these words about dedication:

> In a larger sense we cannot dedicate, we cannot consecrate, we cannot hallow this ground. The brave men, living and dead, who struggled here have consecrated it far above our poor power to add or detract.

Real dedication to anything, of anything, is done by giving, by sacrifice, by offering of something of oneself. As Abraham Lincoln well knew, words do not dedicate: deeds do.

If I want to learn about a particular subject, I go to the expert on that subject. No one can teach us more about dedication than that thoroughly committed person, the Apostle Paul. Here is his insight in Romans 12:1:

> I beseech you therefore, brethren, by the mercies of God, that you present your bodies a living sacrifice,

holy, acceptable unto God, which is your reasonable
service.

***

There are two parts to the Christian's dedication. First,
the motive—the reason behind it—to which the response is
made.

This text of Paul's is of great significance. It is not an
isolated exhortation, a "by the way" remark. It is the pivotal
text of Romans which balances what has been said with
what is to be said. What has gone before is doctrine; what
is yet to come is practice. The doctrine has taught justifica-
tion before God by faith in what He has done. Paul has
been laying out for his Roman readers the marvelous pro-
vision of God's grace; God's wonderful attitude that adopts
us as His children, and gives us the wealth and resource of
a Father's love from which absolutely nothing, not even
death, can separate us. In Moffatt's translation, this section
of teaching culminates with these words:

Who has first given to God and has to be repaid? All
comes from Him, all lives by Him, all ends in Him. . . .
I beseech you therefore, brethren, by the mercies of
God. . . .

Here is the motive for what he will ask them to do. The
mercies of God. God who is Source, Guide, and Goal of all
that is. Nobody has ever given to God first so that God
stands in that person's debt. It is the other way around. Ask
yourself, whence come those talents you use in your daily
business, those instincts for friendship, those capacities for
pleasure? By whose gift have you prospered? By whose gift
has your health been good, your home happy, and your
family dear. By whose gift has life been well worth living?

The answer is that all these have come to you from God. The degree to which He has given them to you constitutes the "you" people know.

It would do none of us any harm to cultivate the habit of attributing life's ordinary daily good things to God, acknowledging also the strength He has given to surmount the world's evil. Remember to say at least in your heart:

Thank God for that work of Monday done, that problem solved; for Tuesday's journey safely made and the welcome at the end of it. For the unexpected smile in the passing, which proved a suspicion false; the pleasure of that book; the chance to help a friend; the comfort of a home on a cold night; for these and a million mercies, thanks be to God! Above all, for the incredible gift, more than words can tell, of God's inestimable love redeeming the world through Jesus Christ our Lord; for this mercy without measure, thank God!

Paul was a person who lived in this way. He was so conscious of the mercies of God that he had given himself completely to God. His life was a psalm of praise. The beat of his pulse, the flash of his thought, the strength of his work, was all of God, through God, and to God. This was the reason why, in spite of circumstances, his life was a constant pageant of triumph, and this was the secret of his calm, unruffled confidence that in all things God was cooperating for good with those who were cooperating with Him.

In the midst of all this, it seems as though Paul thinks of the half-hearted. People like the prodigal son in Jesus' story who have become dissatisfied with the husks of the pig trough in the far country, but who have stopped long before they reached the bread of the Father's house; the

miserable who, while admitting to the claims of God, do
not honor them. They occasionally pull for heaven but
without casting off from shore. Paul speaks to their case
and ours. He connects the doctrine to the duty, the creed
to the character, the theory with the practice. He links the
principle of redemption which he has been proclaiming
with the redeemed life that follows from accepting it. He is
in deadly earnest, saying in effect, "Respond to God's gift,
remember His mercies; this is the motive for all that
follows."

It is not life's kind circumstances that make us Christian,
but the soul's response to the mercies of God. The "set" of
the soul is vital. As the poet graphically puts it:

> One ship turns east, and another west
>   With the self-same winds that blow;
> 'Tis the set of the sails and not the gales
>   Which tells us the way to go.
>
> Like the winds of the sea are the waves of fate,
>   As we voyage along through life
> 'Tis the set of the soul which decides the goal
>   And not the calm or the strife.

"I beseech you, therefore, by the mercies of God. . . ."
Let our response to that motive be like Paul's and nothing
shall drive us off course or overwhelm our spirit.

*
**

If the mercies of God count with us, what must our
response be? The second part of our text—a living gift.

I beseech you therefore, brethren, by the mercies of
God, that you present your bodies a living sacrifice,

holy, acceptable unto God, which is your reasonable service.

Look first at the idea of sacrifice and then at what Paul wants us to sacrifice. Too often, sacrifice is regarded negatively as a matter of giving up this or that. Gag the mouth, blind the eyes, stop the ears and there you have a Christian? Surely not! Christian sacrifice is not a matter of negatively "giving up" but of positively "giving for." Naturally, when one is wholeheartedly "giving for" the glory of God and the good of mankind, lesser things, secondary things, and evil things *will* be pushed out. But this will be a spinoff of a positive attitude. Whoever has this positive attitude will not even call it sacrifice.

Someone once used the word "sacrifice" in connection with David Livingstone's work in Africa. Livingstone, the great Scottish missionary explorer, replied in a letter:

> Is that a sacrifice which brings its own blest reward in healthful activity, in the consciousness of doing good, in peace of mind and a bright hope of a hereafter? Away with such a thought! It is no sacrifice, but a privilege. Anxiety, sickness, danger—these may make us pause and cause the spirit to waver now and then. But let this be only for a moment. All these are as nothing compared to the glory which shall afterwards be revealed. I never made a sacrifice. . . .

But of course he did! His whole life was "given for." Yet the hardness of the sacrifice was lost in the gladness of the spirit that made it. This is what we need to learn. This is *how* we are to sacrifice.

What is the offering we have to give?

It may seem rather strange that Paul should end eleven chapters of perhaps the noblest theological thought ever written by switching from theory to practice in these words, "Present to God . . ." not "your souls" or "your intellects" or "your spiritual natures" but "present to God your bodies a living sacrifice."

This is a good corrective to all highfalutin spiritual notions that do not affect the everyday thoughts, words, and actions of the body. The man or woman who thinks that religion is merely of the spirit: noble ideals, exalted feelings, vague aspirations, and longing faith; and not of the body: sweating brows, outstretched arms, helping hands, and cheering smiles; such a person is misreading the gospel.

One of the greatest lessons of the Incarnation was the honor bestowed by Christ upon the body by His living in it. The Apostles grasped this truth well. In a wide sense they say, "The Church is His body." Every hand that reaches out to heal and steady, uplift and restore is His hand. And in a specific sense they say: "Glorify God, therefore, in your body. Know ye not that your body is the temple of the Holy Spirit which is in you?"

This is a tremendous thought—God active in the world at this moment in the bodies of Christians. For you see, God has chosen to reveal Himself to men and women through men and women. It is in the dedicated body offered back to God as a living gift, that the response of our love to His love is revealed for others to grasp. When we give Him our body, we really give Him ourselves, for the body is the vehicle of the spirit. It is our bodies which through all of our everyday actions shall reveal or fail to reveal the love of God.

True dedication is not simply a matter of writing a bigger amount on a pledge card or mentioning a few ways in which we can help the Church. We may well do such things and it may well be right for us to do so, but they are just the tip of the iceberg. True dedication is giving God ourselves; that great mass of our life spread over work and leisure, our treatment of people, our use of money, our Saturday nights as well as our Sunday mornings, our habits as well as our hymns.

> I beseech you therefore, brethren, by the mercies of God, that you present your bodies a living sacrifice, holy, acceptable unto God, which is your reasonable service.

*
* *

Reasonable service: I consulted seven other translations of these words and they agree that the words mean more than just the proper thing to do. "Service" here really means worship. "Reasonable" would be better translated, "of the reason, of the mind" or even "spiritual." In other words, "Present your bodies a living sacrifice which is the worship of your minds."

There is no more spiritual act than to offer God the living sacrifice of our bodies as the direct outcome of our worshiping mind grasping His love and mercy. Our reason expresses its devotion by surrendering the body to God. Thus the reality of our worship is put to the test in everyday life, wherever our body is.

This is why Jesus' picture of judgment is focused on the body and the mind behind it: on the hand that provided food for the hungry, the voice that welcomed the stranger, the gift that clothed the naked, the feet that visited the sick and imprisoned; and the thought behind them all that made these deeds of the body worship pleasing to God.

For he whom Jesus loved hath truly spoken:
The holier worship which Christ deigns to bless,

Restores the lost and binds the spirit broken
And feeds the widow and the fatherless.

I beseech you therefore by the mercies of God, that
you present your bodies a living sacrifice, holy, acceptable unto God, which is your *spiritual worship*.

For this is the dedication God wants.

———————————

MOST GRACIOUS GOD, lift up our hearts as we behold
your mercies. May we be kindled in a way we have failed to
be kindled before. By your Spirit enlighten and warm us,
that from our fire others may be lighted and warmed too.
Through Christ we ask it. AMEN.